Also by Margie Ryerson

Appetite for Life: Inspiring Stories of Recovery from Anorexia, Bulimia, and Compulsive Overeating

Treat Your Partner Like a Dog:

How to Breed a Better Relationship

Margie Ryerson, MS, MFT

iUniverse, Inc.
Bloomington

Treat Your Partner Like a Dog:
How to Breed a Better Relationship

iUniverse books may be ordered through booksellers or by contacting:

iUniverse
1663 Liberty Drive
Bloomington, IN 47403
www.iuniverse.com
1-800-Authors (1-800-288-4677)

ISBN: 978-1-4502-8159-1 (pbk)
ISBN: 978-1-4502-8160-7 (ebk)

Printed in the United States of America

iUniverse rev. date: 2/2/2011

For my very special pack~

Vic, Laurel, Jen, Mom, and Nelson

Contents

Introduction

"Oh, you are such a love! Come here you sweet thing! Kiss, kiss."

Isn't love wonderful? It's so nice to hear people expressing themselves in such affectionate ways! But too often the recipient of all this devotion is our dog, not our human companion.

We Americans have a love affair with our dogs. Dog care, supplies, and accessories are now a thriving multi-billion dollar industry. There are more than sixty-one million dogs in the United States, and a dog resides in more than thirty-six percent of U.S. households. (We also love our cats, but since cats march to their own tune and don't live to please us the way dogs do, we interact differently with them).

Dog obedience programs are highly popular, and some owners even employ private dog trainers who come to the home to tutor Fifi. There are dog designer clothing lines, dog strollers, doggie day care programs, dog parks, dog hotels with swimming pools and videos in the "guest" suites, dog acupuncturists, dog masseuses, dog psychiatrists, and even birthday parties for dogs. I don't know about you, but if there is reincarnation, I'd like to come back as a dog!

Although we spend enormous time and money to pamper and please our dogs, often we don't put nearly as much time and effort into caring for our domestic relationships. Forty to fifty percent of all first marriages and sixty to seventy percent of all second marriages end in divorce.

Couples workshops often go begging for participants, while dog obedience and puppy training classes are filled to capacity and frequently have waiting lists. We certainly want to establish good relationships with our dogs! More than forty-two percent of dog owners allow their dogs to sleep in their bedrooms, many positioned right between their humans. Isn't that romantic? In my therapy practice I've actually had people say they would rather have their dog in bed with them than their mate!

My husband and I have a three year-old labradoodle named Nelson. Of course he's the sweetest, most adorable dog in the world — oh, that is besides yours, of course. The idea for this book came to me as I returned home many evenings from my work counseling couples. My husband was often in the kitchen, either preparing our dinner or cleaning up. Nelson was right at the front door ready to greet me. I probably spent three or four minutes cuddling and "oohing" and "aahing" over Nelson before turning to my husband to give him a quick kiss and hello. The contrast became almost humorous. Well, for me anyway; I'm not so sure my husband was laughing. I began to think about how I showered so much love and attention on Nelson, and how my husband got the scraps, so to speak.

My work with hundreds of couples as a marriage and family therapist and as a facilitator for couples classes and workshops, combined with my role as a loving dog owner, led me to see parallels between training dogs and humans. I became convinced that many of the same strategies we use to relate to our dogs can improve our domestic relationships.

The most common complaints I hear in my work with couples concern receiving too little attention, time, affection, and positive strokes from each other. In other words, they receive treatment that isn't fit for a dog! If we could only put the same amount of concern and energy into our romantic relationships that we do for our dogs, we would increase our satisfaction with each other, live together with less conflict, and communicate more effectively. Who knows, maybe the divorce rate will decline if we just utter the equivalent of "good dog" to each other more often.

There are a number of excellent books on the market to help couples improve their relationships. Many of the couples I see in my practice tell me they tend to read the first few chapters of these books, then try to apply some of the suggested techniques for a while, before they finally lose focus and abandon their efforts. Just as we must make sure our dogs are alert and well-focused before we train them and expect them to cooperate with us, so must we humans be alert and focused as we try to improve our relationships. And just as we want to keep our dog training techniques short and simple, *Treat Your Partner Like a Dog* is a short, straightforward book with simple suggestions for improving your human relationship.

Do you find yourself practicing any of the following behaviors? If so, maybe it's time to apply some dog training principles to your own relationship.

- You talk to your dog more than you talk to your partner.
- You lavish your dog with more hugs and kisses and cuddles than you give your partner.
- You smile and laugh more with your dog than your partner.
- You plan when and what you will feed your dog, but scarcely consider what you will fix for your partner's dinner.
- You sleep closer to your dog than to your partner.
- You buy toys and treats for your dog, but seldom reward your partner with a spontaneous little surprise gift.
- You worry about your dog's daily exercise, while your partner's health may be compromised with too little exercise and too much food, alcohol, or stress.
- You think how cute your dog looks in a certain outfit, but don't notice if your partner is wearing mismatched clothes.
- When planning a trip with your partner, you immediately wonder if your dog can be included. If he can't come along, your concern for him while you will be gone is greater or equal to your excitement about the trip.
- You take more photos of your dog than of your partner, and your dog's image is prominently displayed on your cell phone or computer.

Now let us look at some of the specific principles of dog training and how you can apply them to your special human relationship. I will illustrate examples using my dog, Nelson, and your dog, "Fifi." I have changed the names and identifying information of the couples in these pages to protect confidentiality. After reading this book, perhaps you will show your sweetheart how much you care by treating him like a dog!

1

Nelson, Stop Chewing My Shoes! (But Aren't You Adorable!)

Accentuate the Positive

My dog is usually pleased with what I do, because she is not infected with the concept of what I "should" be doing.
—Lonzo Idolswine

NELSON IS A BIG GOOFY DOG. He's about three feet high, weighs eighty pounds, and trips over himself daily. He has finally learned to pee like a big boy, but he can't balance on three feet and usually falls into the tree or shrub he's targeted. In the process he sometimes misses and sprays himself instead of the bush. But no matter what strange behaviors Nelson might engage in, I always consider him adorable and lovable.

When I take Nelson to the dog park, here is what happens: I throw a ball for him to fetch. Nelson responds by dutifully bringing back the ball (well, some of the time anyway). We repeat this activity for five or ten minutes. Invariably, each time that Nelson returns the ball, I say "Good job," or "good dog!" Sometimes I even give him a treat for cooperating. We have a certain routine. Let's face it, Nelson is not bringing me money or doing my ironing, yet I shower him with positive attention.

Dog training classes and books instruct us always to look for good behavior and find ways to reinforce it. When we reward our dog for doing something well, he will learn to repeat that behavior over time. In the field of psychology there is a well-known theory called *operant conditioning*. It states that a behavior followed by a reinforcing stimulus results in an increased probability of that behavior occurring in the future.

How often do we use this system of reinforcement and positive rewards with our partner? Do we always offer thanks and gratitude when our partner does the laundry, washes the car, or fixes a tasty meal? Unfortunately, we often take such routine behavior for granted – with our mates, that is, not with our dogs.

Watch dog owners exclaim enthusiastically each time their dog sits or shakes hands on command. A dog could be ten years old and have rolled over many hundreds of times, but she still receives praise every single time. Sometimes we even say sweet, endearing things to our dog for no special reason at all. What a concept!

It's true that taking out the trash doesn't involve a highly specialized skill, (like sitting on command), but perhaps we could thank our mate more often and praise him for some of the small tasks he performs. We may make a fuss when he does something very special for us, like bringing home flowers or throwing us a surprise party, but recognizing some of the daily efforts we make to please each other and to maintain our lifestyles is also important. Remember, too, that handing out praise and appreciation helps increase the likelihood that the behavior will be repeated.

We often tell our dog: "You are SO cute!" "You are SO adorable!" "You are SO pretty?" We are SO complimentary ... to our dog.

But how often do we compliment our mate on his appearance? We may notice when something is wrong, such as hair sticking up or a button missing on a shirt, but how often do we hand out compliments instead of remaining silent or finding fault? In my work counseling couples, it never fails to amaze me how sometimes the simplest shifts in behavior, such as expressing more positive thoughts to each other, can produce dramatic results.

One couple, Mitch and Rebecca, came for counseling because they were angry at each other much of the time. Rebecca felt unloved and unappreciated, and Mitch resented Rebecca's frequent complaints and her lack of interest in sex. He felt he could never please her and that she wasn't interested in pleasing him.

Rebecca grew up in a family where she received an abundance of compliments and praise. Mitch's background was different; both of his parents were reserved and emotionally aloof. Mitch wasn't comfortable giving compliments because he had rarely received them. Even though their early family experiences were dramatically different, both Mitch and Rebecca expected a great deal from each other in their marriage.

In dog training, since most behaviors cannot be learned all at once, we employ a step-by-step learning process called *shaping*. Each step in the learning process is called an *approximation* and is reinforced until the final goal is reached. For example, a dog doesn't immediately learn to shake hands upon command. We need to reward, with either a treat or praise or both, each small attempt she makes toward lifting her paw to shake our hand. Successive approximations, along with rewards, may include telling her to sit, then tapping her paw to get her to move it, then taking her paw to lift it, then instructing her to lift her paw, and so on. (Nelson has learned this trick so well that he now tries to shake hands with both of his paws at once, usually resulting in losing his balance and falling forward onto me).

With our humans, we can practice the same kind of reinforcement. Rebecca's ultimate goal was for Mitch to express appreciation and compliments. Rather than expecting Mitch to suddenly burst forth with a flow of positive comments, Rebecca learned how to employ the concept of shaping. She tried to notice any approximation of the behavior she desired so that she could reinforce it and build on it.

To begin with, she practiced responding quickly to *any* positive comment Mitch expressed. In the past, when Mitch praised her cooking Rebecca didn't count that as a meaningful compliment. She craved compliments of a personal nature, ones that reflected her unique personality or appearance, not just generic praise for following a recipe. But she learned to reward Mitch, with a smile and thanks, for any positive comment he directed toward her, even if it involved her baked chicken. When Mitch received encouragement from Rebecca (instead of her former reaction, "Why do you only compliment my cooking and nothing else?"), he was more likely to repeat the behavior.

Rebecca learned not to take Mitch's lack of positive remarks so personally, and to be more patient with him while he attempted to learn new behavior. Mitch, in turn, was more amenable to the idea of pleasing Rebecca once she became less demanding and critical. Mitch also saw how their sexual relationship improved as he expressed more compliments and appreciation to Rebecca. They had additional issues to resolve, but once they began treating each other more positively, it was easier to work together and to make progress.

If Nelson isn't responding to me the way I want, for example, by ignoring my entreaties to come to me or to lie down, do I pout and sulk and act resentful? Do I complain or yell or scream? No, dog training books instruct me to either try to accept Nelson's behavior, or to figure out ways to encourage him to comply with my wishes. I may employ an incentive approach (a reward), or wait and try again later.

Similarly, we need to approach our relationship with our human in a problem - solving manner. Maybe we will have to accept some of our partner's habits or preferences, just as I accept Nelson's. If my friend, Kathy, could laugh about her dog chewing up the seat covers in her new car, and then laugh again when he chewed up the replacements and four seatbelts as well, maybe we can let go of some of our human's irritating behavior at times. Of course, Kathy didn't exactly like her dog's behavior, and she decided she would no longer leave him alone in the car. But she didn't hold his vandalism against him as she worked on preventing a recurrence.

If we truly want our partner to make some changes, perhaps we need some patience and an incentive plan. Whether the issue is our partner's failure to be on time, to clean up the piles of clothing on the bedroom floor, or to remember special occasions, we will feel better if we have a plan for change. We know that rewarding approximations is important in reaching our goal. The mere act of having a specific goal (i.e., encouraging our partner to be on time) and a plan in mind (allowing her some latitude, telling her to meet you twenty minutes earlier, praising and appreciating all occasions when she is on time) helps avoid emotional outbursts fueled by your frustration and resentment.

Patience is a key ingredient in any successful relationship, canine or human. Many of us seem to demonstrate much more patience with our beloved pup than with our partner. You are most likely patient while walking Fifi until she finds exactly the right spot to sniff and decorate. And you are probably patient when she brings you her ratty toy to play with her for the fifth time in an hour. Even if you don't want to play, you probably let her down gently. How patient are you with your partner when she asks you to repeat what you said or when she is on the phone and you want her attention? Exercising patience is a behavior that we can choose to master if we want. It is within our control.

Having a dog can actually help us increase our patience and tolerance since there are so many occasions where we need to summon these attitudes. Recently Nelson had a little accident on our living room rug. (Not to point fingers – or paws – but I was out of town at the time). Nelson met my husband at the door with a guilty, hang-dog expression and a low, sadly wagging tail. Because my husband is patient and loving with Nelson, after he noticed the stain on the rug he immediately considered what may have contributed to it. In other words, he assessed the situation before he reacted. He realized that he had left Nelson at home for too long and took complete responsibility for Nelson's accident. Accordingly, Nelson received his usual kind and loving treatment.

Can we apply this lesson to our human relationship? How often do we impatiently rush to judgment before we find out all the facts? If our partner forgets to buy some items on our shopping list, or buys the wrong items on our shopping list, (or doesn't come home in time to let the dog out), can we first listen to his explanation before we react? Even if it turns out there isn't a good explanation, you know you would excuse Fifi and give her the benefit of the doubt. How about showing the same mercy for our human?

The more positive interactions we have with our partner, the greater the chance that our relationship will not only survive, but will also thrive. It can be comforting to think that accentuating the positive with our mate is well within our control if we only choose to make it happen. Just as we do with our dog, let's not forget to throw our partner a bone from time to time. We all need to feel special and loved, and to have an occasional treat to chew on.

2

How to Keep Nelson from Wrecking the House

Eliminate the Negative

*I can train any dog in five minutes. It's
training the owner that takes longer.*
—Barbara Woodhouse

WHEN NELSON MAKES A MISTAKE, SUCH AS chewing up a
shoe or peeing on the rug, principles of dog training tell me
that I am supposed to reprimand swiftly at the time of the
bad behavior and then switch gears back to positive mode.
The idea is for Nelson to think of himself as a GOOD dog
and not have a negative self-image. In this way, Nelson will
want to please me because I offer praise and rewards while I
minimize his mistakes. In other words, I don't go back and
rub his nose in it.

If only couples could get over their grievances as easily!
Some of the couples I see in my practice have memories like
elephants when it comes to things their partners did wrong.
Often one person is shocked to find that his partner still
harbors resentment about something that occurred years
ago.

Lydia and Dave had been living together for eight years.

They came in for couples counseling to decide if they should remain together. Three years earlier, after drinking heavily, Dave threw a wine bottle against the wall during an angry argument. He immediately expressed remorse, and soon afterwards he stopped drinking altogether. Dave had never before engaged in violent behavior, and there were no further incidents.

Through the years, Lydia continued to harbor distrust and resentment toward Dave. Her stepfather occasionally beat Lydia and her brother with a belt while she was growing up, and Lydia swore she would never tolerate violent behavior when she became an adult. Gradually she distanced herself from Dave physically and emotionally.

After several months of couples therapy, Lydia was finally able to move past this episode. She saw how her doubts and distrust interfered with any chance for a healthy relationship with Dave. She had been overlooking all of his wonderful qualities while she fixated on this unpleasant incident. Now, like Nelson, Dave would be able to think of himself as a GOOD partner with a more positive self-image. Consequently, the relationship had a better chance to flourish.

If Nelson engages in annoying behaviors, such as barking or whining, I am instructed to avoid giving any attention to him while he is acting up. I don't even look at him. As soon as he is quiet, and there is no barking or whining, I then pay attention to him. This behavioral training concept is called *least reinforcing syndrome*: I want to avoid responding in any way, positively or negatively, to Nelson's misbehavior. The idea is that any response, positive or negative, reinforces a behavior. If there is no response time after time, the behavior will eventually become extinguished.

In our human relationships, the principle of least reinforcing syndrome can be applied when our partner continually does something annoying after we have already asked him nicely to abstain. Say, for example, your honey picks his teeth with a toothpick after eating. You have mentioned your objections many times, (including some polite requests), but he persists in this practice. Following the principle of least reinforcing syndrome, you need to leave the table (calmly) and not return. Busy yourself in the kitchen, or go pick up a book. If you have children, tell them they are excused from the table. Let the tooth-picker sit alone and indulge to his heart's content. Not only will he not have company, but you will be less upset because you have chosen to actively ignore and remove yourself from the situation. If you have dinner guests or are out to dinner, alone or with others, you can still excuse yourself from the table and return when your partner is "behaving."

The following marital conflict illustrates an effective use of least reinforcing syndrome. Married for twelve years, Molly repeatedly experienced anger and frustration when Ken failed to call her when he was running late and wouldn't be home on time. She didn't want to be in the position of having to call to check on him since she felt that it was Ken's responsibility to contact her. Molly tried reasoning with him, explaining how his behavior impacted her, and even promised that, if he would just call her within a half hour after his estimated time of arrival, she would not be mad. Ken usually apologized each time he was late without calling and offered various excuses, but the behavior persisted. In their relationship, Ken was often in the proverbial doghouse.

One Saturday, Molly and Ken planned to wallpaper one of their children's bedrooms together. Molly had lined up activities for the children during this time, and had gathered all of the necessary supplies. Ken was going to his office briefly, but promised to be home by 11am. When Molly hadn't seen or heard from Ken by 1pm, she decided to do something different. Normally, she would seethe angrily while waiting for Ken, and scream at him when he finally showed up. Then she would be in a bad mood the rest of the day.

This time, however, she took matters into her own hands. She was tired of giving Ken's misbehavior so much power and attention. Since her children were at a neighbor's house until 6pm, Molly decided to enjoy the rest of her day. She decided not to leave Ken a note so that he would experience how it felt to be disregarded. Molly took a long walk and then went shopping. She felt good about giving herself this time instead of doing the same old dance with Ken – building up anger while she sat at home waiting for him, releasing the anger at him when he finally made contact, and then continuing to harbor resentment.

Of course, the wallpapering never happened that day, but Molly took a big step in applying the least reinforcing syndrome to Ken's pattern of noncompliance. The results were positive. Molly felt calm and relaxed when she returned home. She had already decided not to start an argument with Ken. Since Ken wasn't berated and put on the defensive, he apologized for not calling and coming home on time, and the next day he wallpapered the bedroom by himself.

Dog trainers encourage owners to be calm and methodical, giving very little negative attention to our beloved dogs. Nelson has learned to expect good treatment and kindness when he is around me. Even during those unpleasant bath times, he gets praise and rewards when he cooperates instead of running away or refusing to budge. If we could just practice this kind of restrained and methodical behavior with our human partner, he or she might also be motivated to cooperate with us more instead of feeling like running away or refusing to budge.

Here is one example of how we can turn a potentially negative interaction into a positive one. Josh and Heather were sitting on their patio one summer evening, relaxing with a nice glass of wine. Heather began to discuss how much she would like to put in a swimming pool in the backyard. Heather often has suggestions for home improvements, while Josh instead worries about their limited financial resources. Josh resents Heather's tendency to suggest new ways to spend their money.

If Josh responds in his typical manner, such as "There you go again. You know we don't have the money for a pool. Why can't you ever be satisfied?" he is reinforcing Heather's behavior, albeit negatively. But if Josh could say something quick and simple, such as "That *would* be nice someday," and then change the subject to how proud he is of Heather's latest efforts to economize or even to how pretty the flowers are that she planted, he offers her positive reinforcement while preserving their nice relaxing interlude on the patio.

Too often, humans do not let things go; instead we harp on our mate and carry on in a negative way instead of switching back to a positive approach as the principles of dog training suggest. Would I (pardon the expression) kick Nelson when he's already down?

How can we handle our partner's annoying and frustrating behaviors? Is there really anyone out there who can just ignore his mate laughing like a hyena or constantly cracking her gum? How about trying to disregard his belching at the table or loud chewing? If your polite requests to stop don't work, you can apply the principle of least reinforcing syndrome and avoid commenting or reacting to the behavior. You will need to calmly take some action to distance yourself from the offensive behavior.

You might choose to use earplugs when the behavior occurs, (keep them handy for these occasions), so that you have more control over your auditory environment. You might remove yourself from your partner by taking your food elsewhere to eat it or by going into another room to make a phone call. If you are still upset and annoyed, you can leave the house and go for a walk or do an errand. The important thing is for you to do something! You will feel better simply by taking control of the situation. Somehow, we are able to address Fifi's irritating traits in a more systematic and less negative manner than we practice with our loved one.

When our partner's behavior isn't merely an annoying trait, but is a full-fledged disagreeable habit, we may get really testy. Some common arguments revolve around financial expenditures, excessive time devoted to an activity, work, or another person, domestic messiness, and childcare and household responsibilities.

Once you let your partner know (nicely, of course) what bothers you and then request that he please correct it, be sure to acknowledge his compliance with your request. If he is cutting back on purchasing electronic devices, let him know you notice and are happy to see this change. If she is now modifying her hyena laugh or putting away her clothes, be sure to express your appreciation.

If you find yourself nagging, stop and think of another alternative. Nagging is not effective because it creates resentment and resistance rather than ongoing cooperation. You might say something such as: "I know I've been nagging you about how long you stay on the computer at night. Is there some way we can work this out? Do you have any suggestions?"

A dog-training concept that can help couples re-focus instead of continuing to harp and nag is called *incompatible behavior*. Incompatible behavior involves substituting a behavior that will make the undesirable behavior impossible.

If the doorbell rings and Nelson constantly jumps up on visitors coming to the door, I don't want to continually apologize and reprimand him. Instead, I can take action. I can spend time training Nelson to sit and even to greet visitors with a toy in his mouth. In this way, he will learn a different behavior when he experiences the stimulus of the doorbell ringing.

With our human, we can apply the principle of incompatible behavior in various ways. If your partner is a speed-demon behind the wheel and you constantly find yourself nagging her to slow down, one obvious solution is for you to drive when the two of you are in the car together. Or you could decide to drive separately. You could look for public transportation options. You could make an agreement in advance to set the car's cruise control device to a designated speed for highway driving. Any of these options will make it impossible for the undesirable behavior to continue.

Erin decided to apply the principle of incompatible behavior with her boyfriend, Jay, who frequently interrupted her when she was on the phone at home. Despite all her efforts to discourage and change his behavior, Jay continued to annoy her in this way. Occasionally, Erin took the phone into the bathroom and shut the door. But she sometimes wanted to fold laundry or do other household chores while she talked, and didn't want to always seclude herself. Erin decided to find ways to keep Jay occupied so she could talk without interruption.

Erin knew that Jay liked to research things on the computer, so sometimes she asked him to look up information for her before she made a call. Or she asked Jay to walk their dogs, or run a quick errand, or do some other activity that would occupy and distract him. The result is that Erin felt more in control; she spent time devising ways to address the problem instead of repeating the same pattern of getting annoyed with Jay. And in the spirit of operant conditioning, Jay began to link the telephone ring as a signal that he should find something to do during that time.

Applying dog training concepts, such as least reinforcing syndrome and incompatible behavior, can give us helpful alternatives to nagging, criticizing, and blaming our partner when we are dissatisfied. Not only are these techniques more effective in the long run, but they also provide us with a rational and systematic approach to keep destructive emotions in check.

Just as I want to make a swift correction with Nelson when I'm displeased with his behavior, we also need to resolve our relationship issues as quickly as possible. The longer we postpone dealing with problems, the more likely there will be deeper resentments and more entrenched behavior. We need to remind and train ourselves to practice techniques for improving our relationship. Is your dog the only one in the household who receives constant praise and a minimum of criticism? If so, it's time to practice treating your human at least as well as your dog.

3

Fifi, Eat Your Yummy Dinner Now!

Communicate Requests and Expectations Clearly

I sometimes look into the face of my dog Stan and see
wistful sadness and existential angst when all he is
actually doing is slowly scanning the ceiling for flies.
—Merrill Markoe

DOG TRAINING PRINCIPLES ADVISE US TO let Fifi know
the rules for behavior early on. Then we need to continue
teaching her the family rules and to expect her to comply
with them. Some of these rules might include: no jumping
up on the couch, no peeing in the house, no jumping up
on humans, and no chewing human belongings. One of
these rules may have an exception; it may be all right for
Fifi to come up on the couch when invited. In this case, we
need to train her specifically for this certain situation. By a
certain age, we expect Fifi to have internalized our rules so
that we won't have to continue repeating them throughout
her adulthood.

Humans live in a much more complex world, of course,
but still we manage to create much controversy over non-
communicated or misunderstood rules and expectations.

Have any of the following situations occurred in your relationship, despite thinking that your mate knew better?

- Your partner extends a dinner invitation to his co-workers without first checking it out with you.
- Your partner tells her parents you both would love to travel and stay with them for Thanksgiving.
- Your partner assumes that you will attend a neighborhood party even though it's being held on a day you have tickets to a football game.
- Your partner buys more new shoes after frequent discussions of credit card worries and obligations.
- Your partner extends his golf game to eighteen holes instead of nine and misses most of your daughter's flute recital.
- Your partner books a "surprise" weekend trip for the two of you on the same weekend your close friend is having her first art gallery exhibit.

These examples are all taken from my experience in counseling couples, and there are many more that could be included. In each instance, one partner made certain assumptions without first checking them out with the other.

As the saying goes, "to *assume* makes an '*ass*' out of '*u*' and '*me*.'" If you frequently operate on the basis of your assumptions, the consequences can be absolutely fur-flying. Even in the case of planning a surprise trip, it may not be enough to find out if your partner has *specific* plans for that time period. You will also need to determine if she has any *pending* plans that are important to her. Otherwise, all of your thoughtful efforts won't truly be appreciated.

If we put in enough time "training" our partner about our expectations and communicating specifically about what we want, we might avoid conflict. Instead, we often think that just mentioning a problem will create change. Sometimes we even assume our partner will know what we want *without* our even mentioning it. Such wishful thinking can put a lot of pressure on a relationship.

When Nelson was a puppy, did I assume that he automatically knew I didn't want him to chew the carpet? Or did I assume that he would stop after a few reprimands? I wished he would learn quickly, and I got frustrated, but I continued to search for ways to train him. I tried to say "Off!" or "No!" as I caught him in the act. I moved him away from the temptation and distracted him with one of his toys to chew. Eventually, I insisted that he learn this lesson, but I gave him time and continuous verbal cues to help him absorb the message. I had specific plans in mind for how to deal with Nelson.

In couple's therapy, I encourage each partner to also be very specific in spelling out what he wants, to listen carefully to his partner's response, and then to follow-up by getting a verbal agreement from his mate that reiterates the terms. In this way, there is no room for misunderstanding. Here is an example of what this looks like:

Andy: "Carol, I want to go to the boat show on Sunday before we visit your parents. What do you think about leaving at 10am, spending two hours at the show, and then getting to your parents' house at about 1pm?"

Carol: "I'm fine with going to the boat show first, but Mom and Dad want us there for lunch and 1pm is a little late. Can we get there by 12:30pm?"

Andy: "All right. Either we can try to leave a little earlier, say around 9:45am, or we can spend less time at the show so we can make it to your parents' by 12:30pm."

This process may seem tedious, and it is! However, let's look at what happens sometimes if we DON"T spell out our needs and expectations:

Andy (thinking he'll go to the boat show on Sunday, but not making his agenda clear): "Ok, so Sunday we're going to your parents' for lunch, right?"

Carol: "Right."

The outcome of this brief and nonspecific check-in is often unpleasant. Each person may think he will get to do what he wants, but no one communicates enough information or tries to form an agreement.

Three-Part Communication

The following is a simple three-part process for communicating a request or expectation:

1. State your request or expectation politely and specifically.

2. Ask your partner for a response to see if he understands what you are trying to communicate.

3. Re-state the terms and ask for a verbal agreement.

Here are examples of how the three-part communication process can help streamline communication and avoid unpleasant surprises:

Incomplete:

Eric: "Wendy, our credit card bills have been huge lately, and I'd like to see if we could cut our expenditures way down for a while.

Wendy: "Okay."

Eric: "Good."

(Wendy then purchases two new pairs of shoes a week later and Eric becomes upset).

Complete:

Eric: "Wendy, our credit card bills have been huge lately, and I'd like to see if we could limit our purchases to only food, gas, and basic supplies for the next three months so we can pay off our existing bills. This means I won't buy anything on eBay, we won't go out to dinner, and you won't go clothes shopping. Would it be okay with you?"

Wendy: "All right, I can do this for three months."

Eric: "So you agree to help me in not adding more to our debt, right?

Wendy: "Right."

Incomplete:

John: "Honey, I've invited Serena and Jim from the office to dinner this Saturday night. I hope that's okay with you."

Amanda: "?X!!###"

Complete:

John: "Honey, I've been thinking it would be nice to invite Serena and Jim from the office to dinner. Is that okay with you?"

Amanda: "Sure, that would be fine. When do you want to do this?"

John: "How about for this coming Saturday night?"

Amanda: "Okay, about 7pm would work. What should we fix?"

Nonverbal Communication

Nonverbal communication accounts for over seventy percent of our overall communication, both with our humans and our dogs. I try to pay special attention to my tone of voice and body language when I instruct or discipline Nelson. I need to think of how to address him: "Sit! Stay! Come here! Good boy! Bring me your toy." I try to make sure my tone of voice matches my message so there is no confusion. I make eye contact and stand up straight so that Nelson takes me seriously. Yet with our partners, our nonverbal communication is often unclear.

It is important to look at how our words, our tone of voice, and our general body language affect communication with our partner. Again, just like with Nelson, we need to pay attention to whether we are being *congruent*, that is, matching up our nonverbal behavior with our verbal message. A common example of a lack of congruence is when our partner displays nonverbal signs of being angry: a scowling facial expression, a tense body, and a snippy tone of voice. However, when we ask if anything is wrong, he says "no."

This is like my telling Nelson "Good dog!" in an angry tone of voice while I glare at him with a mean expression on my face. Even Nelson would know that something was not quite right and would become confused, especially if this pattern of behavior, or *incongruence*, continued. Eventually, Nelson would become anxious and might develop symptomatic behavior of some sort, such as frequently barking or having accidents in the house.

Just like with our dog, confusion in our communication with our partner can ultimately create more damage to the relationship than if the person can just acknowledge being angry. When someone continually gives us mixed signals, we learn that we can't trust that person to be open and honest with us. We will either tend to become very frustrated or we will withdraw; either way, our relationship suffers.

Conflict resolution

When our partner denies that there is a problem but presents body language that reflects otherwise, usually his motivation is to avoid conflict. And because there is power in having the ability to frustrate our partner, sometimes this behavior also reflects a power struggle in the relationship. If your partner frequently behaves in incongruent ways, it is important not to keep "barking up the wrong tree," but to find out exactly what is going on.

When inevitable conflict occurs in your relationship, try to view it as a learning opportunity. A problem-solving approach helps both partners feel more in control and connected to each other. You wouldn't let days or weeks go by before you tried to address Fifi's furniture-chewing behavior, would you? Challenge yourself to try to use effective methods in finding solutions, just as you would if your relationship with Fifi was experiencing difficulty. You would try different strategies until something proved effective. Putting the same effort into your human relationship will help keep it from (pardon the expression) "going to the dogs."

The term "I-message" is commonly used in couples counseling. The idea is to begin your message with the word, "I," instead of "you" so that your partner won't become automatically defensive. If you say, "I wish you would bring me flowers," instead of "You never bring me flowers," you are more apt to receive a favorable response. Starting your comment or request with "you" can sound blaming and accusatory.

I see many people who know this concept intellectually, but fail to use it when they are communicating about emotional issues. Instead of using I-messages, they resort to inflammatory tactics, such as blaming or insulting their partner while trying to make a point. Their goal seems to be more about proving themselves right than finding a mutually agreeable solution. While such venting may feel liberating at the moment, it doesn't accomplish anything other than to alienate your partner and to put even more strain on your relationship.

The first step in trying to resolve conflict is to get a grip on your emotions. Try to subordinate them to your power of reasoning and rationality. You may need some time alone to calm down or to let some days elapse before you attempt to deal with the issue. Maybe you will need to vent to a trusted friend or therapist or write in a journal. Be sure to take the necessary time. Reacting spontaneously and emotionally is not going to accomplish what you want.

Next, think about out how to communicate your feelings to your partner in a way that is both respectful and effective. Be as brief as possible. You don't expect Fifi to respond to long-winded messages. She needs to hear a few key words to understand what you are saying. So does your partner. We all tune out after a while if a message is too long and repetitious.

When there is conflict and strong feelings are involved, the following five-step process can help:

1. Begin your message with an "I" statement with a feeling attached to it. Remember, starting out with the word "You" can immediately kick in our partner's defenses and block

effective listening. Some examples of "I" statements are: "I feel hurt …, "I feel disappointed …," or "I feel sad …"

2. Give a specific example of what your partner says or does that makes you feel this way. "I feel hurt when you criticize my weight …" or "I feel disappointed that you don't spend more time with the kids …"

3. Tell why your partner's words, actions, or inactions make you feel this way. "I feel hurt when you criticize my weight because I *am* trying to eat better and exercise." or "I feel hurt when you criticize my weight because I already feel bad enough about myself without having you join in too."

4. Make a specific request that will help you. "I feel hurt when you criticize my weight because I am trying to eat better and exercise. Would you please not say anything from now on?" or "Would you please give me compliments instead of criticism since that's what would really help?"

5. Obtain your partner's agreement with your request. If he isn't willing to agree to your request, find out what he *will* agree to that will help you feel better about the situation. In the example above, maybe he finds it difficult to express a compliment, but he will agree to refrain from criticizing your weight.

Now let's look at some common accusatory messages and see if you can "leave it" and instead apply the five-part method of communication:

Old: Sheila: "Craig, you never spend time with me anymore. All you care about is work."

New: Sheila: "Craig, I've been feeling lonely lately because you've been putting in long hours at work. I miss spending time with you and am wondering if we could set up a weekly date night together? Do you want to do this? … Great! Which night shall we pick?"

Old: Tim: "Why do you always have to back-seat drive?"

New: Tim: "I feel annoyed when you back-seat drive because it makes me think that you don't trust my driving. Would you please stop doing this? … All right, I'll agree to stick to the speed limit if you'll agree not to tell me how to drive."

Old: Patti: "Can't you ever put your clothes in the hamper? I'm sick of picking up after you."

New: Patti: "I feel upset when you don't put your dirty clothes in the hamper because it seems that you're not thinking about me and how it makes more work for me. Could you please pick up after yourself? … Thanks. That would make me feel better."

Just as we put effort into determining exactly what we want our dog to do or not do, it is certainly possible to be more specific with our humans. We practice ways to communicate with Fifi until both human and dog have mastered the task, and we need to do the same with our human. We can avoid making assumptions about what our partner thinks or wants. We can communicate as specifically as possible and work toward forming an agreement with each other. We can practice congruent communication so that our verbal message matches our nonverbal message. And we can think in advance how to structure our dialogue with our partner so that we can be more effective. The five-part method of communication is a model for clear and respectful interaction. After all, none of us want to be in placed in the doghouse for failing to communicate adequately. We want to be understood by others, and especially by the most significant person in our pack.

4

No, Nelson, the Remote Control is Not Your New Chew Toy!

Foster an Attitude of Cooperation and Respect

*"One reason a dog is such a lovable creature
is his tail wags instead of his tongue."
Unknown*

"THESE ARE MY MASTER'S SLIPPERS AND I must not chew them," is the taboo we try to instill in our canine housemates. But our human partners are often harder to train. In a human relationship, the following instances of failure to cooperate happen all too often:

"I always forget to fill up the gas tank. Oh well."

"I didn't notice the dishes were dirty. Besides, they can wait until tomorrow."

"I know you are worried about money, but I needed to buy a new necklace to lift my spirits."

"I don't see why you can't put down the toilet seat yourself. Why do I have to remember?"

I am training Nelson to respect my property and my territory, and I set limits. He's learning that he has to share *my* shoes with *me,* since after all, I'm the one who needs to wear them to work in order to earn money to buy him his dog food. And if he digs in the yard, he has to be hosed off before he comes into the house – and the hose is not his friend.

In order to instill respect in Nelson, I first must decide what is important to me. Then I need to figure out ways to communicate my messages to him. For example, if I want him to stay out of the kitchen while I am cooking, I train him with approximations and positive reinforcement to respect my boundary. I reward him when he sits in an adjacent room and watches me, rather than his preferred activity of sticking his nose up onto the kitchen counters to check for anything edible. Over time, I continue to offer intermittent praise or treats to reinforce the desired behavior. Again, this is a calculated effort – well thought out and purposeful – to achieve my goal.

Unfortunately, many couples struggle with issues of control, and do not respect each other's limits or share possessions or territory equitably. One person may try to dominate the other in ways we wouldn't tolerate with our dog.

Anne and Greg came in for counseling during their second year of marriage. Each was previously married and divorced. Anne had two teenage daughters who lived with them, and Greg had one grown son who lived and worked out-of-state. Anne and Greg had not lived together during the three years they were dating, but when they got married Greg moved into Anne's house.

Although they were highly compatible during their years of dating, both Anne and Greg found that combining households produced difficult challenges. They reported arguing constantly, even about trivial matters, and resentments were skyrocketing. Each felt that the other either couldn't or wouldn't see his point of view. They had not had sex in three months, and both were questioning their decision to get married.

Many of their issues involved matters of cooperation, respect, and control. Anne stated that Greg was trying to impose his will and change the way she lived, and she resented it. She had many decorative pieces throughout the house that she collected from her travels or had received as gifts. Greg complained that the house was much too cluttered and often criticized her decorations and use of space.

With two teenagers in the house, Anne was somewhat relaxed in her expectations for a neat and clean environment. Greg, however, had different standards for home care and maintenance. He complained that Anne didn't respect his feelings because she let dishes pile up in the sink and stacks of items collect on the dining room table. He was especially upset when Anne's children left their possessions all over the house, and Anne did nothing to correct them.

Anne said that Greg had some behaviors that bothered her, but the only one she refused to tolerate was when he disciplined her daughters. Greg had a good relationship with Anne's daughters before the marriage. The couple agreed that after they married Anne would continue being in charge of handling disciplinary issues with the girls. Now it seemed that Greg was asserting himself more and more, to the point where both of Anne's daughters were becoming increasingly alienated from him. Even when he didn't say anything, his body language made his dissatisfaction obvious.

This couple had become locked in a power struggle. Each felt the other was being unfair and insensitive. Each felt right and that the other was wrong. As we have seen, it is rarely a case of one person being right and the other wrong, but it often takes some intervention to realize this.

Before we try to solve this couple's problems, let's look at my relationship with Nelson once again. Along with training Nelson to respect us and our way of doing things, my husband and I also show him respect. We buy him the kind of food he likes (supplemented occasionally with tasty scraps and treats), we search for toys he can enjoy, and we consider his daily schedule and his need for companionship and exercise. Nelson is eighty pounds of scruffy dog, so we draw the line at letting him sleep in our bed at night. But many dog owners do relent and let their pups sleep with them in their beds, exactly where they please.

We expect Nelson to cooperate with us, and we also cooperate with him. If we're lying comfortably on the couch watching TV and he brings us a toy to throw for him — an activity that seems to happen every ten seconds — and he appeals to us with his soulful puppy-dog eyes, we often give in and play with him. And sometimes, when we know he would enjoy even more play time, we rouse ourselves to take him to a dog park or on an outing. All in all, the relationship is mutually beneficial.

Now, let us consider our human couple, Anne and Greg. At this point in their relationship, they are not doing much to please each other or to consider each other's needs. They are locked into tracking how often and in what ways their partner is failing to comply with their wishes. They are more intent upon keeping a mental score of wrongdoing than in finding ways to cooperate with each other. As Nelson might say, what a doggone shame!

In order to help establish more respect and cooperation, Anne and Greg first had to understand the issues underlying their need for control. We spent many sessions examining their history in each of their families of origin and first marriages. Usually, numerous control issues signify a strong fear of being overwhelmed, hurt, or disregarded and discounted. Often, those who try the hardest to control their environment are the very ones who had little control in prior years of their lives.

In order to try to modify their controlling behavior, Anne and Greg each agreed to jot down their angry and resentful feelings in separate notebooks, along with 'H" for hurt, "O" for feeling overwhelmed or overpowered, and "D" for feeling disregarded. I asked them to wait until we met each week to share these feelings with each other so that we could explore them constructively. Gradually, they began to recognize the triggers that lay behind their attempts to control each other. Each realized the need for power in the relationship was really a response to fear – of being hurt, overpowered, or discounted; their struggle for control with each other was more of a defensive reaction than a true desire to take over.

Once Anne and Greg were able to understand themselves and each other better, they were more motivated to find ways to accommodate each other's needs. As with dog training, we needed to go back to the basics before we could proceed any further. If in training and disciplining Fifi, we shout at her, pull painfully on her leash, or drag her outside, she will develop either a fear reaction or become more aggressive than we would like. Either way, she will not be ready to cooperate with us. We will need to re-establish consistent positive reinforcement with her and eliminate punishment over time, so that she will learn to respond favorably.

Anne and Greg's relationship needed similar rebuilding. Their first task was to increase positive interactions and decrease negative ones. We wouldn't think of insulting or criticizing Fifi when we're with her, would we? After all, we certainly don't want to damage her self-esteem. We are very protective of her and her feelings. We need to apply some of this same concern and good will to our special human too.

After such a lengthy period of arguments and criticisms, it took time for Anne and Greg to make the necessary corrections in their behavior. They first needed to catch themselves in the act of misbehaving. Self-awareness is usually the starting point in making any behavioral change. Then they could proceed to substitute positive comments and behaviors for negative ones. Anne and Greg each agreed to try to "catch" the other in the act of saying or doing something positive and to express appreciation whenever this occurred.

After many months of continuous effort, both Anne and Greg were very encouraged. Each felt much better about their relationship, their partner, and themselves. As a therapist, this is the true payoff – helping couples abandon their sense of hopelessness and replace it with optimism and joy.

Now let's look at how you can apply some of these methods to your own relationship. First, let's take another look at Nelson and his training. Here are some ways I know if Nelson is taking too much control in our household, the dog equivalent of trying to get us to roll over without even offering us a treat:

- He inserts his face next to ours at the table while we are eating dinner.
- He barks at us inside the house to try to get us to play with him.
- He pushes past us to greet people at the door – and then proceeds to jump up on them. (We need much more work on this one, now that I think about it!)
- He sneaks naps on the sofa at night. (Hmmm, we *really* need to work on this one too!)

I need to establish certain desirable behaviors with Nelson and maintain a good working relationship with him. I don't want to shout at him or control him by being aggressive or mean. I need to be able to tell him "no" when he approaches me to play with him, in what seems like every sixty seconds, without hurting his feelings. He has learned about "not now" and "later," so we can cohabit peacefully.

Dog-training techniques in the past utilized tough measures, such as loudly "barking" orders at the dog and using physical force at times. Modern dog-training techniques, while still exacting, are more moderate. They recommend establishing a cooperative relationship with our dog so that he knows exactly what is expected of him. Then he can more likely behave in a calm, controlled, and consistent manner.

The same is true with humans: We can work together better if we know what we expect of each other. And it is helpful to communicate with each other without barking or growling. Here are some ways you can tell if you or your partner – or both of you – are trying to take control in your relationship instead of working together:

- Frequently exhibits a volatile and intimidating temper.
- Is physically abusive. You must leave this relationship quickly and find a safe place to go.
- Is emotionally abusive. Your partner often ridicules, accuses, belittles, insults, and embarrasses you. He or she preys on your feelings of inadequacy and insecurity. This relationship requires professional intervention to determine whether or not it can be repaired. You and your partner will each need individual therapy as well.
- Strictly controls financial expenditures and makes all important decisions.
- Engages in withholding behavior. He or she is uncommunicative, aloof, and unaffectionate.
- Always assigns blame to you without taking any responsibility for his or her mistakes.
- Exhibits passive-aggressive behavior. Passive-aggressive behavior is a pattern of expressing negative feelings indirectly and often obstructively instead of addressing them openly. A person who behaves in a passive-aggressive manner seems agreeable to others' requests and expectations, but he doesn't follow through. He uses nonverbal behavior to express disagreement or anger that he can't or won't express

verbally. By passively resisting others' requests or demands, he derives feelings of satisfaction and increased control.

Some examples of passive-aggressive behaviors are: frequently "forgetting" important occasions such as birthdays, anniversaries, or children's school plays or athletic events; frequently "misunderstanding" prior agreements and, for example, immediately purchasing a new motorcycle when the agreement was to wait a year; agreeing to clean up a cluttered room but letting it go for weeks or months; being chronically late or failing to show up altogether for appointments, social plans, or work; agreeing to stop buying new clothes and then hiding new purchases in the back of the closet; and neglecting to do one's share of agreed-upon yard work or purposely doing an incomplete job.

If you observe controlling behavior in your partner, it helps to avoid direct confrontation. Use "I" messages, as we discussed in the previous chapter, to report what you are seeing, how it makes you feel, and what you would prefer that your partner say or do. See if he or she is willing to help you out with "your problem."

Timing is important. Try to pick a neutral time to express yourself, when the two of you are getting along well. Many couples say that they don't want to spoil the good mood by bringing up an unpleasant subject. However, this is exactly the right time to approach your partner with a tactful "I" message. If you wait until you are arguing and the atmosphere is tense, emotions will be high while motivation to listen and cooperate will be low.

One enhancement to an "I" message is called a "soft

start." Usually, if one person begins his or her message calmly and lovingly, the outcome is more apt to be positive.

Let's look at a sample conversation as Sam tries to raise an important issue with his wife, Polly. Polly has a history of being a controlling, "high-maintenance" person. Sam has usually deferred to her wishes, but he has begun to resent her demands and his own meekness. Sam and Polly are home alone one afternoon while their children are at their grandparents' house. Sam has waited to talk until they could be alone and relatively relaxed. He opens his message with a soft start.

Sam: "Sweetheart, I really like to please you, and I hope you realize this. I know you love good jewelry and sometimes I feel pressure to buy it for you when I don't think we can easily afford it. I want you to be happy, but I don't want to have to worry about how to pay for expensive gifts. Do you have any ideas that can help?

Polly (pouting and being controlling): "I can't help it if I have good taste and happen to like expensive jewelry. I guess you can just buy me a toaster for my next birthday instead."

Sam: (trying to be conciliatory and use humor to diffuse the situation): "Good idea. Maybe I can find a jewel-encrusted toaster for you. Seriously, though, I'm wondering if we could limit my jewelry gifts to one per year, either for your birthday or for Christmas? What do you think?

Polly: (acting like a martyr) "I *guess* so. Sigh."

Sam: (ignoring Polly's theatrics since he got the agreement he wanted): "Great. I'm glad you're being understanding. I appreciate it."

One couple I worked with presented a real challenge. Katie had passive-aggressive tendencies and Todd displayed strong withholding behavior. What this meant was that neither one communicated in an open and honest manner. They were engaged in a power struggle without even recognizing it. Katie's sweet demeanor camouflaged her determination to prevail and get her way. Todd's remote, indifferent attitude enabled him to stake out his territory and avoid conceding to Katie.

As an example, Katie was in the habit of correcting Todd in front of people. When they were at dinner with a group of friends, she would lean across several people at the table to "correct" something Todd said. Katie spoke in a soft, loving tone as she contradicted Todd. Todd would seem like he was shrugging it off, but Katie's insensitive behavior was really alienating him. The more aggressive she became, even while ostensibly being sweet on the surface, the more Todd withheld his thoughts, feelings, and affection from her.

This couple took many sessions to be able and willing to disclose their true feelings to one another. When Katie was growing up, her parents were strict and demanding. They didn't let her express herself. If she tried to disagree with them, she was punished. As a teen, Katie developed passive-aggressive behavior as a way of resisting their authority. She pretended to agree with her parents and then secretly did whatever she wanted. Todd grew up with a single mother who often lost her temper at Todd and his brother. Todd developed a pattern of retreating to his room and withdrawing from conflict. Invariably, his mother would feel guilty and try to make amends with him. In this way, Todd was able to exert some degree of power in the relationship.

Once Katie and Todd understood their own behavior and each other's, they could better avoid falling into the same trap, the hidden power struggle. They learned how to honestly and openly discuss issues that bothered them. Their fears of being overpowered by the other were eventually put to rest as they gained the closeness that comes from working together.

Dog trainers will verify that some "problem" dogs would be wonderfully obedient and cooperative if only they were handled properly. But if their owners mistreat them, physically or verbally, these dogs will not respect and respond well to their masters or to any humans. Some may even become vicious.

For couples, this problem of "negative handling" is often played out in their sexual relationship. One partner behaves indifferently, or is verbally or physically abusive toward his mate. He may offer only negative attention, pointing out when things are wrong, rather than providing support and compliments. He may go further and insult, ridicule, or even push, slap, or throw things. Typically this person is the male in the relationship, although sometimes it is the female. The couple comes in for counseling because they are not getting along and are close to separating. Their sexual relationship is infrequent or nonexistent.

The partner who is emotionally distant, insulting and/or abusive wants more frequent sexual relations and complains that his or her partner is not responsive. Complaints escalate into anger and resentment. The problem is compounded as the angry partner blames and accuses his mate in a misguided attempt to show how wrong and unfair she is being. He expects her to see the error of her ways and to fix the problem. If there is no resolution, sometimes the resentful partner will act out by having an affair or by forming an emotional attachment to someone else.

This relationship conflict becomes a vicious cycle. Let us

take a look at a very common situation in the case of Marcy and Will, a couple with two young children who came in for help with their marriage. For several years, Will had tried everything he could think of to convince Marcy to have sex more often. On average, the couple had sex about once every month, and often Marcy was a reluctant participant. Will wanted to have sex at least twice a week, and he also wanted Marcy not only to be enthusiastic, but also to initiate sex sometimes.

Upon closer examination, Marcy also wanted to *feel* like having sex more often than once a month. She wished she could be more responsive to Will and derive more enjoyment from their sexual relationship. But there were several roadblocks. She felt mistreated and abused in their relationship and had a great deal of hostility toward Will. These feelings were certainly not the recipe for a happy relationship, sexual or otherwise.

When Marcy and Will first met, they felt very compatible in every way. As time went on, and children entered the family, they naturally had more responsibilities and less time for each other. When Will wanted to feel a closer connection to Marcy, he would initiate sex. He assumed Marcy would respond positively when he indicated a desire for sex, since he knew she loved him. Marcy, however, like many women, first needed some "emotional foreplay." Sex manuals describe the importance of physical or sexual foreplay as a prelude to sexual intercourse. That's all well and good once a couple have both agreed to have sex. But for some couples, arriving at the decision to have sex can be problematic.

For Marcy, "emotional foreplay" included having Will hug her, hold hands when they were out, compliment her appearance and personality, and not just behave in these ways in order to have sexual relations. These behaviors needed to stand on their own.

Marcy had explained her needs to Will many times and how she would be much more receptive to his sexual overtures if he could be more affectionate and complimentary. Instead, Will took offense and felt that Marcy was trying to tell him what to do instead of accepting him for who he was. He felt that he showed her he cared by what he *did* for her – working, sharing household and childcare responsibilities, helping her care for her widowed father, and suggesting weekends away and vacations.

Not only did Will refuse to comply with Marcy's repeated requests for some basic romancing, but he also became angrier each time Marcy turned down his sexual advances. Initially, he accused her of being frigid and selfish. Over time, he became more physical and yanked the sheets off the bed or knocked over the lamp on Marcy's nightstand in fits of temper. He threatened divorce and wondered why anyone would ever want to be with someone like her. The more Marcy refused to have sex with him, the more Will lashed out with negative and unloving behavior. Will was definitely barking up the wrong tree if he thought these tactics would ever succeed.

This couple became locked in a negative spiral and needed intervention to change their patterns of dealing with each other. First of all, Will needed to work on anger management techniques in separate individual therapy sessions. He agreed to stop berating Marcy and to stop behaving in a physically aggressive manner when he became hurt or angry. He had not touched Marcy in anger, but at times he had lashed out explosively with objects. As long as Will exhibited any kind of abusive behavior, nothing would be able to be accomplished.

Marcy would not be able to develop the necessary trust in him to sustain a relationship.

In addition, Will agreed to read books on the differences in men and women's physiological responses and sexual motivations. He agreed to eliminate negative comments about Marcy's sexuality and to try to substitute some of the behaviors Marcy had requested. Both partners agreed not to have sexual relations for a period of three months while they came in for weekly counseling sessions. They needed this time to take some pressure off their relationship and to create some positive interaction with each other.

This couple had much more work to do in their therapy sessions, but their case illustrates how the way we elicit cooperation and respect in our human relationships is similar to how we function with our dogs. When our partner and dog feel *our* respect for *them*, they are much more willing to please us in turn. The use of criticism, threats, and physical force undermines relationships and leads to a lack of cooperation and respect.

Take a minute to think about your own relationship and whether or not you and your partner show each other respect on a regular basis. When you have differences of opinion, do you still respect each other's viewpoint? Do you have admiration for certain qualities your partner possesses? Do you think your partner is an ethical, caring individual? Do you and your partner allow each other the ability to be separate individuals with your own thoughts, needs, and interests? Having respect for your partner and feeling respected in return increases the likelihood of having a cooperative relationship.

Think about how well you both cooperate when decisions need to be made. Do you share in decision-making or alternate so that one person doesn't predominate? Do you each make an effort to see your partner's position? Can you discuss sensitive, controversial topics with each other relatively peacefully without blaming, attacking or criticizing? And can you suspend some of your personal reactions so that you and your partner can adopt a problem-solving approach when needed? Consider how you can show more respect and cooperation in your relationship. Often, if one partner is willing to demonstrate more effort, the other becomes more encouraged and positive as well.

Fifi loves it when everyone in her household is cooperating and getting along. She smiles more often and wants to cuddle or play. It's a doggone shame that she can't figure out how to help us get along as well with each other as we do with her. That's for us to try to figure out so that everyone's tails can wag happily in our homes.

5

Fifi, You Really Do Need to Eat Your Yummy Dinner Now!

Follow Up Words with Action

"Never repeat a command. Most dogs are not deaf; they just choose not to listen."
—Connie Jankowski, Dog trainer

IF NELSON DOESN'T HEEL UPON COMMAND, I pull on the leash to get his attention. If he continues to jump up after I've said "off," turning my back to him sends a strong message. If he is not listening to me well enough, ignoring him, putting him outside for a "time out," or spending time retraining him are all possible plans of action.

Similarly, when our partner becomes angry or defensive about an issue, and nothing we say makes a difference, taking action can be helpful. Sally had been married to Don for over thirty years. Their children were grown and living on their own. In recent years, Sally had reduced her hours working as an architect to three days a week. She was eager to spend more time sharing interests and travels with Don. She asked him if he would be willing to spend more time with her in the evenings and on weekends, and he agreed. However,

Don, an attorney, continued to work late many evenings, and also continued to sign up for various professional seminars and volunteer projects. Sally felt lonely and discouraged as she waited for Don to make time for her.

The couple had many arguments while Sally tried to convince Don to be sensitive to her needs and desires. Finally, in exasperation, she thought of a creative solution to the problem. She decided to rent a room, on a month-to-month basis, in a nearby house of single professionals. Sally reasoned that if Don was unwilling to provide companionship, she would surround herself with other people who could provide her with interaction. Sally also decided that when Don wanted to see her, he would need to visit her in her new quarters or suggest plans to go out together.

It is important to note that Sally took this action in a calm, non-angry manner. It was a natural outgrowth of her need for companionship, but she didn't want to alienate Don; rather, she wanted him to miss her and appreciate her more. During the months Sally rented the room, she enjoyed talks and occasional dinners with her roommates. She made plans with other friends, and Don initiated contact several times a week. Sally enjoyed her time with Don and felt like they were dating again. She no longer felt unappreciated and taken for granted as she looked for ways to take more control over her life.

Not surprisingly, Don developed a new appreciation for Sally when he realized she wasn't at home and available when he wanted. He took her more seriously. After several months, Sally and Don worked out a mutually agreeable arrangement to spend time together, and she moved back home. Sally's decision to take action, instead of continuing to complain, led to a satisfying outcome.

One of the most frequent complaints I hear from couples is on the issue of nagging. Typically, the male casts the female in the role of being an excessive nag. But often neither partner realizes that the male usually nags about certain things too; only his nagging comes out more in the form of complaints or criticisms.

The good news is that you *can* teach an old dog new tricks after all. Fifi, for example, will learn to tune you out if you repeat yourself over and over. Why bother listening the first time if she knows she'll hear the message again? There is no incentive to pay close attention. But you can work on training her to listen the first time.

For example, if you first get Fifi's attention, set down her dinner, and tell her it's time to eat, you don't need to repeat yourself. If she doesn't begin eating her food within five minutes or so, remove it, and then try again later. She'll realize at some point that she's better off grabbing the opportunity when it presents itself the first time. (I know that certain dogs will devour food whenever it is offered to them, but others, like Fifi and Nelson, may be a bit fussier).

If you find yourself nagging frequently (or complaining or criticizing), think about what you can *do* instead. Of course, first you need to try the communication techniques we discussed in previous chapters. However, if your partner is highly resistant to verbal messages of any kind, no matter how endearing you make them, it is time for a different approach.

Here are a few examples of what you can *do*, rather than repeat yourself over and over:

Problem:
Cindy is constantly upset that Evan leaves piles of

paperwork and magazines on the floor in the bedroom. He becomes enraged if she threatens to move anything, and he constantly checks to make sure all of his papers are "in order." Cindy hates confrontation, and continues to try to persuade him to clean up his mess. She has tried all possible verbal strategies to address the problem with him.

Solution:

Cindy buys a large basket that can accommodate all of Evan's papers and magazines. One day she puts everything into the basket. Evan, of course, is furious when he discovers this, but let's not forget that Cindy has also been furious for quite some time. When Evan sees that Cindy is determined to have her reasonable wishes respected, and that she is willing to back up her words with action, he grudgingly concedes. He is not happy about the new arrangement, but Cindy needs to remember that she wasn't happy for a long time either. Happily, it turned out that Evan's "bark was worse than his bite," and he eventually adapted to the concept of a clutter-free bedroom floor.

Problem:

Bob was raised to be on time, and he even tried to be early as often as possible. His girlfriend, Susan, however, didn't share his attitude about time. She frequently arrived between ten to thirty minutes late for their get-togethers, including dinners out, movies, and hikes. She always called him to say she was running late, but that wasn't the point; Bob wanted her to be punctual like he was. Bob and Susan lived thirty minutes away from each other, so sometimes it was necessary to meet when they wanted to see each other.

Bob was frustrated and angry that Susan persisted in her habit of being late, no matter what he said.

Solution:

Bob was clear that he loved Susan and wanted to make their relationship work. Susan agreed that she wanted to try to be more prompt, and that it wasn't fair to keep Bob waiting so often. She admitted that her lack of punctuality was a longtime bad habit.

With the help of their couples therapist, Bob let Susan know that if she didn't arrive within fifteen minutes of the agreed upon time, whenever possible he was going to start without her. This meant that he would leave her movie ticket at the box office and go sit down by himself, and it would be up to Susan find him inside the movie theater. Or, similarly, he would go sit and start watching the ballgame instead of waiting outside the stadium for her. If they were meeting for dinner, he could choose to order and begin eating when the food arrived. This wasn't optimal, of course, but at least he wouldn't feel quite so resentful.

Some activities, like walks or hikes, couldn't be modified in this way. Bob would bring something to read, or use the time to contact people or go online on his iPhone. The important change for Bob was that he would be prepared, either by starting an activity without Susan, or by planning something to do while he waited for her.

Although Susan wanted to change, Bob realized he couldn't make that happen; only she could. And his complaints and criticisms when Susan was late only put them both in a bad mood. Now Susan would have the opportunity to work on changing her behavior without nagging and pressure from Bob.

Problem:

Jenny and Steve, a couple in their forties, had two elementary-school age children. Jenny's problem was that Steve's cousin, Phil, invited himself to stay with them for several days every few months. Phil lived in another state, and he owned a business that required him to make sales calls in their area four or five times a year. In order to save money, rather than stay at a hotel, Phil would call Jenny and Steve the day before he was due to arrive and announce that he was coming. If they had plans or other houseguests, he would put a sleeping bag down on their living room floor. He took advantage of their hospitality, never bringing a gift or contributing to a meal. He never offered to help. In addition, Jenny objected to his foul language in front of the children and his cynical attitude toward life. All in all, the visits quickly became an ordeal for her.

Jenny had long ago asked Steve to set some limits with Phil about the frequency and length of his visits, as well as what was expected of him as a guest. She wanted Steve to say "no" sometimes, that it wasn't convenient for Phil to stay with them. Steve refused to speak up, however, and argued since Phil was *family*, he should be made to feel welcome and comfortable whenever he visited. Steve would then get angry at Jenny for having a "bad attitude." Jenny felt that Steve cared more about Phil and his needs than hers. Over the years, Jenny and Steve had spent a great deal of time and frustration arguing about this situation, and Jenny grew increasingly furious.

Solution:

Jenny finally decided to take action since talking to Steve hadn't accomplished anything. The next time Phil announced he was coming to stay, Jenny made plans with friends to go out to dinner the first two nights he was visiting. She fed the kids dinner, and left Steve in charge to help with homework and bedtime, and to fix dinner for Phil and himself. Phil stayed one more night, and Jenny asked Steve to pick up Chinese carry-out for dinner. She left the dishes in the sink after dinner.

In addition, Jenny told Steve that he would need to make up the spare bed for Phil, and that he was in charge of laundering the sheets and towels. In other words, Jenny refused to participate in any of the extra work required for Phil's visits. Since she hadn't been consulted beforehand, she decided it wasn't her responsibility. As she detached herself from the situation, Jenny felt less like a victim and more in control; it was a huge relief to her.

Not surprisingly, Steve got a clearer picture of his cousin when he was the one directly responsible for him.

Now that he had to deal on his own with Phil's selfish and inconsiderate behavior, he realized that Jenny's feelings were justified. Eventually, Steve initiated a discussion with Jenny to determine how to handle the issue of Phil's visits. They decided to limit them to once a year for two days only, telling Phil that having him come to stay more often required too much extra work for them along with their jobs and children.

It is important to learn to trust your instincts to determine if your partner is treating you fairly. Many people question themselves and their feelings so much that they wind up denying there is a problem in their relationship. They dislike conflict and negativity, so they convince themselves that they are expecting too much from their partner. They manage to suppress their frustration until the next problematic situation arises.

Here is how a dog lover learned about the importance of trusting her instincts. Mara adopted a small mutt from her local animal shelter. Corky was about three or four years old, and there was no information on his history. Corky seemed very docile, sweet, and shy. He responded well to Mara when she visited him, and she decided he would be a good companion for her. Mara was in her twenties and lived alone in a condo that she owned. The first few months went uneventfully as Mara and Corky established a relationship with each other.

Then, Mara's brother came to stay with her for a few days. Corky, who had never reacted negatively to men while playing in a park or walking in the neighborhood, suddenly began to growl and bare his teeth in an aggressive manner whenever her brother, Randy, was nearby. Corky's behavior was very unsettling for Mara. She tried to smooth things over by having Randy offer Corky treats. Corky would tentatively approach Randy, grab the treat, and then go off into the distance to continue growling at him.

Then, Mara thought more about the problem. Randy was an average-size man, but he had a loud, deep voice. Perhaps Randy's voice was scary for Corky. After all, Mara had no way of knowing what kind of treatment Corky had received from people in the past. Maybe Randy reminded Corky of someone who had threatened or mistreated him. She urged Randy to use a softer, higher-pitched voice when he was around Corky to see if that would make a difference. Sure enough, Corky responded differently when Randy altered his voice.

Mara's instincts, on behalf of her dog, proved to be extremely helpful. Not only did Mara learn how to help Corky when her brother was around, but now she knew what Corky needed in other situations as well. Mara could have ignored the problem and told herself that Corky would be back to normal as soon as her brother left. She could have convinced herself that, of course, an adopted dog was bound to have some problems, and she would just have to tolerate Corky's annoying and difficult behavior at times. Instead, she chose to think through the problem and to take steps to solve it.

In the following case, Anna ignored her instincts in order to keep the peace in her marriage. By the time this couple came in for counseling, the damage had already been done. During their four-year marriage, Anna had always trusted Gavin to take care of their finances. Their paychecks automatically went into their joint bank account, and Gavin paid all the bills. Over time, Anna began to notice interest charges on their credit card. Gavin assured her that, although he had gotten a little behind with the payments, he would catch up within the next few months. He became angry at Anna for questioning him, so Anna let the matter drop. When she checked the credit card balance after a few more months, the interest charges had mounted. Anna again questioned Gavin about the charges, and this time he became enraged, saying she didn't trust him and that she was trying to micro-manage him.

Anna became alarmed about this change in Gavin's behavior and began observing him more closely. She usually went to bed by 11:00 p.m. while Gavin stayed up late, playing games on the computer. What Anna discovered was that Gavin wasn't just playing mindless computer games, but that he was gambling on a poker site. By the time she confronted him about the problem, Gavin had lost over $12,000, much more than they had in savings. While Anna was naturally worried about how to handle the huge debt, she was most upset about Gavin's betrayal of her trust.

This couple had a lot of work to do to repair their relationship. One important step they took was for Anna to assume responsibility for their finances. Gavin was remorseful and agreed to get help for his gambling addiction. Anna learned that she needed to confront Gavin more forcefully when she sensed something was wrong, and not be intimidated by his anger. She continued in individual therapy to learn how to be more effective in her marriage and in other areas of her life as well.

Nelson has a large sheepskin bed that he usually finds quite comfortable – until we're asleep that is, and then he sometimes makes his way to the couch. We tried pointing to the couch and telling him "off" and "no," but that didn't work. In the morning we still found couch pillows dislodged onto the floor and long tufts of white dog hair on the cushions. We even caught him in the act in the middle of the night several times, and purposely tried to scare him by waking him up suddenly. That tactic worked for about two days. Finally, in desperation, I covered the couch with books from our coffee table to make it an uncomfortable alternative to his bed. Yes, this finally worked. The only problem was that I now had the chore of putting away massive numbers of books in the morning and then remembering to replace them on the couch again in the evening. Somehow, this seemed like a hollow victory.

Upon consulting web sites, books on dog training, and friends with dogs, I finally concluded that Nelson needed a more comfortable bed. I ordered him what looks like a mini-couch of his own, and we'll see if this makes a difference. In this way, too, dog training and human relationship building are very similar. Both are ongoing, never-ending processes that we keep attempting, with various degrees of success and failure. If we don't want our furniture or our relationships "going to the dogs" we need to keep looking for solutions that will help.

Taking action can be encouraging and empowering. There many possible strategies to use when you have exhausted verbal requests and pleadings with your partner. You can try different ideas to see what works best for you and for your relationship. If you are able to reduce much of your frustration and resentment by taking action, and if your partner eventually responds, you will know you are on the right path.

6

Nelson, Why Can't You Be Well-Behaved Like the Cocker Spaniel Next Door?

It Sometimes Helps to Lower Our Expectations

"Folks will know how large your soul is,
By the way you treat a dog!"
—Charles F. Doran

IF WE HAVE A CHIHUAHUA, WE don't expect her to run long distances with us. We don't expect our Great Dane to sit on our lap and cuddle with us on a chair. We know we are barking up the wrong tree if we want to enter the scruffy mutt we just adopted from the pound in professional dog show competitions.

When we got Nelson, our labradoodle, we knew his temperament was open and friendly to all. We didn't expect him to be a dog that would guard the house and protect us. Actually, he *does* try to jump on strangers when they enter our house, but only to shower them with nose nuzzles and affection. One reason we got this breed of dog was because they are hypoallergenic and don't shed. So the long white hairs we found on our clothes and furniture were a definite surprise. But because we love Nelson, we developed tolerance toward the unexpected dog hair that adorns us and all of our possessions.

We love and accept our dogs, no matter what their idiosyncrasies may be. Certain traits may bother us at times, but we try to be tolerant and adjust our expectations. Dogs can drool, smell, whine, bark, barf, dig, eat our flowers and shoes, you name it – and we will still be devoted to them.

Can we say the same thing about our human? Do we try to be tolerant and adjust our expectations? Do we try as hard to do this with our partner as we do with our dog?

In the early stages of a romantic relationship, we appreciate each other and observe our partner's good points. Because we are attracted to the person, we are not focusing on weaknesses and flaws. Some couples are able to remain complimentary and positive toward each other without interjecting negative attitudes into their relationship. However, many couples leave this "honeymoon" period and move into the next phase where they attempt to change and "improve" each other. The glass can start looking half-empty after a while, and definitely in need of a refill.

There are certain fundamental requirements for any loving relationship: respect, consideration, trust, cooperation, enjoyment, and a willingness to make sacrifices for each other. But not everyone masters all of these qualities perfectly, and this means our partner will sometimes fall short in one or more of these areas. We don't want to lower our expectations too much since that would be self-defeating. So we need to find the right balance. We may have kissed our share of frogs before finding our prince or princess, only to discover that our prince leaves the toilet seat up and our princess doesn't hang up her clothes.

Sometimes the very qualities that initially attracted us

to our partner become unappealing to us over time. For example, if you fell in love with your sweetheart's gentle, unassuming nature you can't expect this person to suddenly become a take-charge person. One couple I worked with had this very dynamic. Rick was shy, quiet, and had a relatively passive personality. His wife, Becky, was a human dynamo, with lots of energy and an upbeat attitude. Rick and Becky worked well together for many years until their children grew up and left the nest. Alone with each other after twenty-three years, Becky began to resent Rick's quiet nature. She missed all the commotion of family life and felt bored and unfulfilled in her marriage.

The more Becky tried to push Rick to talk to her, the more withdrawn and silent he became. He knew that Becky wasn't satisfied with him, and he felt increasingly inadequate. His lowered self-esteem caused him to become more withdrawn and quiet. A vicious cycle had developed.

Over time, Becky realized that she needed to find more outlets for herself instead of suddenly expecting Rick to satisfy her social needs. As Becky began finding more fulfillment in old and new friendships and activities, Rick stopped experiencing pressure from Becky to change. As a result, he felt more at peace with himself and in their relationship. He was able to go back to being a thoughtful and kind source of support for Becky. And Becky made a concerted effort to value the qualities in Rick that had helped sustain her throughout their relationship. In our dog parlance, Becky realized it was fine for Rick to remain a retriever instead of expecting him to suddenly transform into a mastiff.

A common complaint I often hear in my therapy practice is that one or both partners don't feel truly accepted by the other. We hear a lot of talk about how important it is to be kind and accepting of ourselves, and also tolerant of our faults. In this way, we increase our self-esteem and confidence. The same principle applies in our relationship: If we provide an attitude of acceptance toward our partner, our connection with each other will be enhanced and strengthened.

One couple whom I saw for over two years had gotten into the pattern of finding fault and trying to change the other. Marlene and Darryl lobbed blame back and forth as they each tried to prove their point. Instead of looking for positive qualities in each other, they focused on what was wrong. Their relationship deteriorated into frequent shouting matches. Incidentally, this couple often brought in their five year-old dog, a little Pekingese named Heidi. In between bouts of reporting wrongdoing by the other, both Marlene and Darryl would pet and cuddle with Heidi. Guess who got most of the treats in this family?

Both Marlene and Darryl came from families where conflict and arguments were the norm. Marlene's parents divorced when she was nine, and Darryl's parents were also divorced before his father died. Neither had witnessed how to be positive and supportive in a marital relationship. They had one child, age eight, and the couple shared that they were also too critical and negative with him at times.

In order to break this cycle of fault-finding, Darryl and Marlene needed various interventions. Simply talking about this issue and then resolving to change would not be enough. To begin with, I asked Darryl and Marlene to each make a list of their individual strengths and weaknesses. Not surprisingly, both partners identified many more weaknesses in themselves than strengths. When a person doesn't feel good enough about himself, he will tend to project his dissatisfaction with himself onto his partner. It helped for

Marlene and Darryl to understand some of the reasons behind their negative interaction with each other.

Next we worked on ways they each could change their own ratio of strengths and weaknesses. Each partner was assigned the task of helping the other improve his self-image. For example, Marlene felt inadequate when she hosted friends in their home. She worried about the appearance of the house, her clothes, her hair and make-up, as well as the taste and appearance of the food. As a result, although she would have liked to do more entertaining, she rarely did.

It was Darryl's assignment to figure out ways to help build Marlene's confidence. He suggested that she consult a personal stylist to help her go through her wardrobe, and to analyze her hair and make-up. In the process of making this suggestion, he offered Marlene reassurance that she always looked good to him! That alone was a huge breakthrough.

Darryl offered to help more with housework, and to step up his efforts in the days preceding any social occasion at their house. In addition, he thought of ways to take emphasis off of the food they served. He agreed to grill an entrée and vegetables, so that Marlene wouldn't feel so much pressure. He suggested that she buy a dessert from a bakery if she was too worried to prepare it herself. Both agreed that they wanted to entertain more, and that Darryl's ideas would probably help a great deal.

Next, Darryl picked something from his list that he wanted to change. He wanted to lose twenty pounds and get in better physical shape. In the past, Marlene had nagged and criticized him about his weight. Her methods produced the opposite effect of what she wanted; Darryl was more determined to resist Marlene's pressure than do anything about his weight.

Now Marlene understood the necessity to provide encouragement and support instead of criticism. She agreed to help Darryl by preparing healthy meals when it was her turn to cook. She also agreed to go hiking with Darryl once a week and to help clear out an area of their family room where he could keep some exercise equipment. Marlene also wanted to lose some weight and increase her physical stamina. By working together this couple was able to not only help each other, but also to grow closer as they pursued their common goal.

Just as we do with our dog, it helps to look upon our partner with an attitude of acceptance and good will. If we are frequently mean and negative with Fifi, she will be unhappy and unresponsive to us. If, instead, we focus on her good points and build upon them, she will flourish. Training and helping Fifi doesn't just happen; we need to analyze the situation and figure out how we can be effective. It is not possible for Fifi to change her behavior all on her own, just as it is difficult for our partner to make changes without our cooperation. When we improve our own attitude and behavior first, we can then help both our human and dog relationships thrive.

It is interesting how we can usually tolerate Fifi's flaws more easily than our partner's. Here are a few examples:

- Fifi barks in the early morning (at a squirrel outside? at dust mites in the air?) and wakes us out of a deep sleep. All is forgiven as we get up and start our day earlier than we had anticipated.
- Our mate snores occasionally and wakes us out of a deep sleep. We complain, accuse, and harbor resentment.

- Fifi doesn't come snuggle with us when we'd like her to because she is more interested in gnawing on her rawhide bone. We think about how adorable she is.
- Our partner doesn't want to snuggle with us when we'd like him to and we are hurt and angry.
- Fifi decides to come snuggle with us after all. The only problem is that she is full of mud from her romp in the dog park, and we are now covered in filth.
- We are at the ballgame with our human sweetie and he accidentally spills his beer all over our clothes. We lecture him about his carelessness and sulk for at least three innings.
- Fifi's breath smells like an animal carcass. We laughingly mention this from time to time, but don't actually do much about it.
- Our honey's breath smells like an animal carcass. We are grossed out and constantly complain about it to her.
- Fifi chews up one of our favorite slippers. We are momentarily upset about this. Then we add this transgression to our repertoire of amusing Fifi tales.
- Our human sweetie is often careless while doing the laundry, and the color of one of our favorite white sweatshirts is now pink. We are upset for a long time about this, and add this transgression to our repertoire of grievances we harbor against her.

I took Nelson to puppy-training classes faithfully. He followed the lessons our stern instructor barked out, and, I'm proud to say, he was one of the top members of his class when he "graduated." Then we were on our own. One day when we passed by another dog on one of our walks, Nelson yanked the leash, jumped about five feet high, and tried to run after the dog. I felt like I was holding onto a wild stallion. Where had all the classes, the money, and the time and effort spent on training gone? It was discouraging to say the least. My high expectations that Nelson would be an exemplary dog in every way were shattered.

Five minutes later, I had already made a complete recovery and I was back to thinking of Nelson as my wonderful, beloved dog. Why is it so much easier to adjust our expectations with our canine than with our human? If we could learn to give our partner more leash, so to speak, our relationship could be so much better!

Here's an example of how our human couple can reduce expectations for a happier outcome: Elizabeth had a close girlfriend, Alison, whom she had known since childhood. Alison was a loud, opinionated person who tended to dominate conversations. Elizabeth loved her for her kind heart and loyalty. However, Elizabeth's partner, Lily, had a difficult time being around Alison and sometimes became sarcastic and impatient with her.

Elizabeth asked Lily if she would promise to be nicer to Alison the next time the three of them were together. Lily agreed to try to be polite and agreeable. However, the following month when they were out to dinner together, Lily directed several sarcastic remarks to Alison. Later, Elizabeth was furious at her; after all, she had just promised not to do this very thing.

Here is where Elizabeth's reaction can make a difference in her relationship. She could choose to be right or she could choose to adjust her expectations slightly and be effective. If she chooses to be right, she can incite a major confrontation with Lily about her behavior and broken promise. If she lowers her expectations, however, she can discuss the problem with Lily in a calmer manner. She can explain how upset she was that she let her down and ask her how she could avoid doing this again in the future? Her reasonable attitude can create more motivation for Lily to make a change than if she blows up at her. And, at the same time, Elizabeth can feel better and more in control by remaining calm.

Why should we be less forgiving of our partner than we are of our dog? Canines and humans both need practice and reinforcement before we get things right. Sometimes we humans just need to work more doggedly before change can occur.

Psychologist Dan Wile addresses the issue of expectations in his book, *After the Honeymoon: How Conflict Can Improve Your Relationship.* He writes, "When choosing a long-term partner ... you will inevitably be choosing a particular set of unsolvable problems that you'll be grappling with for the next ten, twenty, or fifty years." He advises accepting this inevitability and trying to figure out how best to deal with the problems that are part of every relationship.

In some instances, it helps to lower our expectations of some of our partner's basic personality traits and not just his or her behavior. When he met Leanne, Greg was initially attracted to her compassion for people and her gentle nature. After fourteen years of marriage, however, he had become weary of being the one in their relationship to take care of the inevitable problems in running a household. Whenever there was a charge on a bill that needed contesting, or a problem with a warranty, or with a hired workman, Leanne depended on Greg to handle it. She hated conflict of any kind and went to great lengths to avoid it.

Greg had every right to feel frustrated and besieged. He hadn't envisioned that these tasks would always fall on him to handle. However, he also knew that Leanne's timid personality made it difficult for her to take the initiative. He could either put pressure on Leanne to change, or he could adjust his expectations of her. If he applied pressure and Leanne was unable or unwilling to change, their relationship would suffer. If, on the other hand, he lowered his expectations by realizing that Leanne's unassuming and gentle nature was what first attracted him to her, he could decrease his resentment and frustration. When change is unlikely, we can work on developing greater tolerance and acceptance of our partner.

Just as we appreciate Fifi for the wonderful dog that she is, so we can appreciate our mate for all of his or her special qualities. When Fifi is unable to fulfill our every need we remind ourselves that, after all, she is only a dog. Likewise, we need to tell ourselves that our partner is only human. Each species has its limitations, and we will be happier and more satisfied if we can adjust our expectations.

7

Fifi, I've Already Thrown You the Ball Two Hundred Times Today

Spend Time Together and Play Together

"Dogs are our link to paradise. They don't know evil or jealousy or discontent. To sit with a dog on a hillside on a glorious afternoon is to be back in Eden, where doing nothing was not boring – it was peace."
—Milan Kundera

AT MY LOCAL DOG PARK THERE are dog owners who bring their dog two times a day to play. These conscientious people often interact with their dogs by throwing or kicking balls for them to retrieve. We're not quite as dedicated as these folks, but we do walk Nelson each day and provide play opportunities with other dogs when possible. And we play with him often at home. After all, who can resist those huge puppy dog eyes and slobbery stuffed animal in his mouth to be pulled and tossed? Most dog owners are very aware of their dog's need for companionship and play.

Now let's compare the time we spend on our dog's recreation with the time that we devote to our partner each day. Conversation is our human equivalent to the interaction we have with our dog. One study estimates that the typical American couple spends less than two minutes per day in *meaningful* conversation. Agreeing on pizza instead of Chinese for dinner is an important decision of course, but it isn't considered meaningful conversation. Neither is who is going to the T-ball game on Saturday and who is going to play golf. What *is* meaningful is sharing on an emotional level with each other – worries, joys, concerns – and expressing mutual caring and concern.

Fifi's needs are a high priority, and we feel guilty if we don't spend enough time with her. After all, she *depends* on us for play and fun. But between work, household responsibilities, children, volunteer projects, religious commitments, friends, and recreation, many couples don't make enough time for each other. And unlike with Fifi, too often there isn't even a twinge of guilt when we don't have time for our partner; we just expect him to understand that our time is limited. We may take our relationship with our partner for granted because we are so busy devoting time to other people, activities, and even to our dogs.

We know that friendships require time to develop and maintain. We know that our children require a great deal of time and attention. But we may try to justify to ourselves that "quality time" with our partner is an adequate substitute for "quantity time." The truth is that our relationship needs both quality and quantity time to keep functioning at a healthy level. Not only do we need to make enough time to share with each other and enjoy each other's company, but we also need to make time to regulate inevitable conflicts that arise.

"Let's play! Go get the ball! It's time to go for a walk!" All of these messages make our dog excitedly snap to attention.

How often do we say similarly enticing things to our partner? Instead, our conversations often center on the leaky roof, our headache, or in-law visits. No wonder our first tendency is to tune each other out instead of perking up our ears like Fifi. She's waiting to hear about her next good time or treat, while we're expecting to hear about the next garbage pick-up or what is wrong with the car.

Dr. Howard Markman, Co-Director of the University of Denver's Center for Marital and Family Studies, points out the importance of spending time together and having fun: "The more you invest in fun and friendship and being there for your partner, the happier the relationship will get over time. The correlation between fun and marital happiness is high, and significant."

How do we find the time for our partner in our already busy schedules? It won't just happen unless we make it happen. One study found that the average couple goes four weeks between dates with each other.

Many couples long for the earlier days of spontaneity when they could have an idea and quickly implement it. One couple I know, both successful professionals, were married for nine years before having their first child. When their baby was two weeks old, they suddenly decided it would be fun to go out to a movie. As they were gathering up their belongings and getting ready to leave the house, it suddenly dawned on them that they now had a baby asleep in the other room! They hadn't yet come to the realization that their days of spontaneity were on hold for quite a while.

In relationships, spending time together is what really matters, not whether or not the time is spontaneous or planned. The more complex our lives are, the harder it is to be able to pick up and go. We need to adapt to our changing lives by looking ahead and carving out time for our relationship.

Weekly or bi-weekly date nights with our partner help give couples a consistent way to spend time together. The knowledge that the date night is approaching can help sustain couples through occasional days of limited communication and contact. This time with each other can be happily anticipated and cherished, so that couples avoid taking each other for granted.

It is also important to have time away together several times a year, even if it is just for a long weekend. Getting out of our routines can refresh and strengthen our relationship. We share new experiences together and create memories, and most importantly, we make opportunities to have fun together.

Do you walk Fifi on the same path day in and day out? Or do you look for new and interesting places to walk and play with her? Many dog owners take their dogs on trips and vacations with them to enjoy their company and vary their routines. Even Fifi gets into a rut at times and enjoys a break.

Find Interests to Share

Some couples struggle to find mutual interests to share. One person may be passionately devoted to gardening while her partner may prefer hiking and backpacking in his spare time. I often hear couples in my office complain about each other's use of spare time and choice of hobbies. Conflict can arise if neither wants to join a partner in his or her interest.

Often the solution lies with developing a new interest together. Research studies show that taking part in challenging and novel activities can boost a couple's sense of love and satisfaction. There are so many activities from which to choose, and merely planning for a new pursuit can breathe life into a relationship. Sharing an outside activity provides a couple with a mutual frame of reference, more interesting topics for discussion, and the opportunity to explore different facets of each other. Couples get to see each other in a different light, one which typically enhances the relationship.

The concept of *outside activity* is important. I have had couples say that the main activity they share is watching certain television shows or videos. They think that enjoying the same type of home entertainment is sufficient for maintaining a close and vibrant relationship. While watching television and movies can certainly be fun and relaxing, and is perfectly fine in moderation, the main problem is the *passive* nature of this activity. Yes, you are appreciating what you are viewing together, but you are not challenged to interact with each other or to communicate in a personal way. If your recreation time with each other typically leads to conversations about "those Ravens," or "those Giants." or the latest sitcom or reality show, it is time to branch out.

Maintain an Emotional Connection

Marital research points to loneliness in marriage as the primary factor in divorce and extra-marital relationships. To help maintain an emotional connection with each other, researcher Dr. John Gottman recommends that couples incorporate the following rituals into their daily life:

- Partings: Before leaving for work, share at least one interesting thing with each other that will happen during that day.
- Reunions: In the evening, have a "How was your day, dear, conversation." Sharing events and thoughts from your day with each other can help manage stress and provide needed emotional support.
- Appreciations: Find a way each day to genuinely communicate affection and appreciation toward your spouse.
- Affection: Kiss, hold, and touch each other. Play is good. Make sure to kiss each other before going to sleep.

All in all, experts recommend spending at least forty minutes a day communicating with your partner. Some conversation can be by phone if necessary, but texting, tweeting, and online conversations aren't adequate substitutes for eye-to-eye contact. Ask yourself whether Fifi is content just hearing your voice on the phone? No, she thrives on being with you in person, hearing you speak to her, and having you scratch and cuddle her. Many dogs cock their heads when their owners talk to them, trying to understand what they are saying. For both humans and canines, there is a sense of safety, security, and emotional well-being when they are in close proximity to their loved ones.

Improve Communication

Certain communication methods help couples connect well with each other. These tools are an essential part of relationships but are all too often ignored. We have already discussed "I messages" and some ideas for resolving conflicts. Now we need to look at basic conversational techniques. One of the most important concepts is *active listening*.

How many times have you or your partner asked each other "Did you hear what I just said?" or "Why aren't you listening?" and had the response "I heard everything you said." The reason you asked the question in the first place was because your partner didn't behave in a way that indicated he was listening. Perhaps he was flipping through television channels or maybe he looked at you but had no expression on his face – possibly because, although he may have *heard* what you said, his mind was elsewhere.

Active listening takes place when the listener *shows* he is listening. This is why it is called active listening rather than passive listening. The listener makes eye contact with you, and he comments on what you are saying or asks questions. In other words, he participates in the dialogue so that it is a verbal exchange and not just a monologue. By actively listening to what you have to say, he shows genuine interest and caring. It is a vital and powerful component of effective couples' communication.

A goal of active listening is to hear your partner's words and perspective without interruption and without judgment. You allow him the freedom to explore his thoughts and feelings. You offer your opinion only if your partner requests it or if you ask him first whether or not he wants it.

Another aspect of active listening is how you reply to the message you have heard. We have all witnessed young children's conversations with each other that bounce back and forth with little or no acknowledgment of the speaker's message:

Child A. "I got a new bike for my birthday."

Child B: "I went to Disneyland for MY birthday."

Child C: "MY birthday is next week and I want a new puppy."

Unfortunately, some adult exchanges sound similar to those of young children. Too often the listener may be thinking of what he wants to say next instead of focusing on the message from the speaker. Or he may tune into the words in the message but not absorb the larger context, such as the speaker's expression, tone of voice, inflection and emphasis. Perhaps your partner's actual words sound fine, but his facial expression seems worried and sad. It helps to notice and address all of your partner's messages, both verbal and nonverbal.

Think of how you respond to Fifi when you interact with her. Not only do you talk to her and establish eye contact, but you also notice her body language. Is her tail up or down? Is she wagging her tail or not? Is she looking at you or are her eyes downcast? What sounds is she producing? Communication with Fifi can be effective and complete because you pay attention to all of her signals and responses. Challenge yourself to notice your partner's body language more frequently so that your human relationship will also thrive.

Some mental health professionals recommend not going to bed angry. While this is an admirable goal, I do not think it is always possible or realistic. We all need our beauty sleep, not to mention how difficult and awful it feels to have to function the following day with little sleep. I have heard from couples who have literally stayed up most of the night discussing and arguing in order to avoid going to bed angry. Unless you can wrap up the conflict within a reasonable period of time, I recommend agreeing to revisit the issue the next day or as soon as possible, at a mutually convenient time. Yes, this means you may go to bed harboring hostility or resentment or hurt, and it may be difficult to sleep. But if you know that there is hope for some resolution the next day, perhaps you can set aside some of your emotional anguish and "sleep on it."

Schedule Time for Each Other

Scheduling time for each other may seem rather business-like, but making this effort ensures that it will take place. Couples may have good intentions, but often other compelling activities or people (or dogs) interfere.

I recommend that couples calendar a small amount of time each week to sit down for planning sessions. You can plan for time to be together that particular week and also develop plans for future weeks. In other words, both short-term and long-term planning on a regular basis is important for couples. Without this, you run the risk of taking each other for granted and forgetting to incorporate time for each other into your schedules. Or you may find yourself devoting time to other people and situations that suddenly arise instead of setting aside some vital time for each other.

A side benefit of establishing planning time is that *both* partners put in effort. I often hear one person in a relationship complain that he or she has to do all the work to find ways to spend time together. The person who always has to initiate may feel slighted or neglected, and often suffers a decline in self-esteem as a result. This imbalance can lead to hurt and resentment over time. But if you agree to plan together and add this planning time into your weekly schedule, both partners will then be responsible for making things happen.

Spending more time together can help increase the sense of fun, adventure, and sharing in your relationship. It is important to feel a sense of connection and mutual purpose with your partner. When you're experiencing a deep bond with each other, you're better able to deal with problems and unexpected setbacks, both in your relationship and in other areas of your lives. If you fail to relate on a deep enough level with each other, the potential for conflict can increase and satisfaction with the relationship may decrease. One of the primary causes of infidelity in a relationship is a desire for more fun and excitement. Just as you try to make sure Fifi has enough fun in her day-to-day life, be sure to check on your human relationship's fun quotient too.

And speaking of fun and sharing in relationships, Nelson enjoyed a special bonding experience with his close buddies. He and three dog friends were invited to their friend Tahoe's birthday party. The dogs enjoyed special ice cream cups made expressly for dogs, games, and party favors. The idea for the party came from Tahoe's six-year old owner, Mike, and his mom actually held the party for her son's sake. But the twist here was that this birthday party for Tahoe was a *surprise party*! Mike thought it would be fun to surprise Tahoe, so we were instructed not to breathe a word to our dogs ahead of time. Keeping the secret was hard, of course, but we all managed! Since dogs have such acute hearing, we were unable to sneak up on Tahoe in the schoolyard to actually surprise him, but we tried anyway. Needless to say, Tahoe was touched by the outpouring of such love — and licks, wrestling, and chasing. Much fun and joyful barking was had by all.

Wouldn't it be nice to bring this sense of playfulness and joy to our human relationships so we can have more good times together? By making time for each other on a daily basis, sharing interests, and engaging in fun activities together, you can give your relationship a positive boost. And by practicing active listening while sharing these moments together, you will experience a greater sense of closeness with each other as well.

8

Nelson, I Love You So Much!

Express Affection Verbally and Physically

"When the Man waked up he said,
'What is Wild Dog doing here?'
And the Woman said,
'His name is not Wild Dog any more,
but the First Friend,
because he will be our friend
for always and always and always.'"
— Rudyard Kipling

"Who's my favorite snookums? Kiss, kiss, kiss!" But wait ... we're talking to Fifi again! By the time we finish lavishing Fifi with affection, sometimes we don't have much left for our human. Yet, just as our relationship with Fifi thrives when we bestow affection on her, so does our relationship with our partner.

One of the most common complaints among the couples I work with is that they don't receive enough verbal and physical affection from one another. Typically, women want their partners to be more complimentary, appreciative, and affectionate. Men often want more appreciation and more sexual interaction. When these needs are fulfilled, both men and women are better able to feel good about themselves and their partners. They feel closer and more emotionally connected.

Show Verbal Affection

We have discussed how Fifi is often the one in our household who receives the most praise and enthusiasm. Not only do we praise Fifi daily, but we do it effusively. "Fifi, you brought me the ball again! What a GOOD DOG!!!" or "Fifi, you're so ADORABLE!!!"

Verbal affection can take many forms. It can consist of a "honey" or "sweetheart" thrown into your sentence. It can be affectionate teasing that is well-received by your mate. It can be words of appreciation for your partner's deed, effort, caring, support, or simple presence. It can be compliments on any aspect of your partner's appearance, personality, behavior, or performance. It can be positive reminiscences of happy times spent together. It can be an "I love you," or "I'm lucky to have you in my life," or "I can't wait until we can be alone together."

Expressing affection verbally can have two significant effects for a couple. The obvious one is that the receiver of the message is pleased and encouraged. But the second effect is that the *sender* derives pleasure and positive feelings from delivering the message. Each partner regards the other more favorably after a positive interaction. So exchanging positive messages is really a win-win situation for both members of a couple.

Dr. John Gottman, author of *The Seven Principles for Making Marriage Work*, discovered that couples who have five positive interactions to one negative interaction are more likely to last. His research also concludes that when the ratio of positive to negative interaction is 1:1, the divorce rate increases dramatically.

How to implement a positive ratio is the challenge for many couples, especially if you have gotten into the habit of focusing on each other's faults. Think about how vigilantly you may catch your partner being wrong or careless, and how quickly you let him know.

Nelson gets to revel in lots of praise, even when he has been a ... shhhh ... bad boy. When Nelson wonders off in the park and pays no attention when we call him repeatedly, how do we talk to him when he finally decides to make his way back to us five or ten minutes later? Amazingly enough we tell him, "Good boy, good dog," lots of good words. We may even give him a treat to top it all off because he finally decided to head our way. We make many allowances for our beloved Nelson, but not as many for our beloved humans.

Exhibit Physical and Sexual Affection

Touch is a basic need for humans and also for many animals. Over fifty years ago, psychologist Harry Harlow demonstrated the importance of physical contact and comfort in his experiments on baby rhesus monkeys. He removed the infants from their mothers and gave them a choice between a cloth mother and a wire mother. The monkeys clung to the cloth surrogate mother whether or not it provided them with food. When the monkeys were later divided up between the cloth or wire mothers and given bottles of milk, the ones who had the wire mother had more trouble digesting the milk and more frequent diarrhea. Harlow concluded that the lack of contact comfort was psychologically stressful to the monkeys.

Similarly, studies of infants in orphanages by psychoanalyst Rene Spitz pointed to the importance of touch and physical comfort in addition to emotional comfort. Babies and children who were deprived of these vital caretaking behaviors developed symptoms such as depression, anxiety, emotional disturbances, and in severe cases, a failure to thrive resulting in malnutrition and death.

Research has uncovered the beneficial physiological and mental effects of touch. Touch, including kissing, produces increased levels of a calming hormone called oxytocin. This natural hormone helps reduce anxiety, heightens feelings of well-being, and strengthens the immune system. Touch can often help lower blood pressure and dissolve headaches. Frequent touch has been shown to improve problem-solving ability and alertness. Lack of touch, or "cutaneous deprivation," can lead to emotional disturbances, decreased intellectual ability and physical growth, reduced sexual interest, and a weaker immune system.

More and more, we are hearing about the benefits of massage therapy as a stress reducer and immune system strengthener. Not only is massage recommended for humans of all ages, but for dogs as well. In her book, *Bonnie Bergin's Guide to Bringing Out the Best in Your Dog*, this dog expert claims that "dogs respond to touch as eagerly as people. Massage helps both you and your dog to feel good together, which clearly promotes the intuitive connection critical to a healthy relationship. Also massage can help dissipate resistance, calming the dog and making it more open to paying attention to you and your needs."

Some of my favorite times with Nelson are in the mornings when I wake up and he is still resting comfortably in his bed. (Since Nelson is a really big boy, eighty pounds and five feet in length from upper to lower paws, we all sleep more comfortably when he uses his own bed!) We are a perfect match since neither of us is a morning person – or dog. Sometimes Nelson is sprawled on his back, limbs extended, in what looks like a really uncomfortable position. But he snores softly and doesn't budge despite voices, or the coffee maker, and other usual routines of our morning. This is the time I love to softly massage him. When I apply the right touch, he becomes mesmerized, like a lizard when its belly is stroked, and he is perfectly still for a long time. I can tell he is calm and content, and luxuriating in this physical sensation.

All too often physical expressions of affection are neglected in human relationships. Many couples fondly remember how physically demonstrative they were with each other in the beginning of their relationship, when they couldn't stop touching, kissing, and cuddling. There was also more sex and passion. While it may be difficult to sustain this level of physical interaction over time, it is still possible — and important — to demonstrate affection physically.

In my therapy practice I hear many women complain that they don't feel as sexually turned on to their partners as they would like. Some have very little interest at all in having sexual relations with their partner. Men, on the other hand, express feelings of hurt, resentment, frustration, and/ or anger that their partners don't appear to be interested in sex. They complain that they always have to initiate sex, and that often their partner comes up with excuses and refuses to participate.

Sometimes there are biological problems that interfere with a couple's sexual functioning, such as hormonal imbalances, medications, or diseases. Sometimes there are psychological influences that interfere, such as sexual abuse, cultural and gender messages, and body image issues. And sometimes, other problems in the relationship need to be addressed and resolved before progress can be made in the sexual arena. Here are some of the issues and behaviors that can interfere with the expression of affection in a relationship:

Roadblocks to expressing verbal and physical affection
Fault-Finding

Frequently, the reason behind couples' fault-finding tendencies with each other is nothing more than pure habit. And as with all habits, if you want to make a change and are willing to put in effort, you will ultimately be able to succeed. It will take agreement from both members of the couple to change this particular habit, however. That is because one partner's fault-finding tends to produce a similar response from the other partner. Negativity breeds more negativity, and a cycle becomes established.

If you are in the pattern of finding fault with each other and agree that you each want to change, the first step is to become aware of each negative message that is transmitted. Some families have a jar for cursing where the offender agrees to put in a certain amount of money for each infraction. It is possible to set up this same kind of system when partners make negative comments to each other. Or a couple can select a code word, such as "buzz" (as in buzzer for a wrong response), or say pointedly, "Would you please repeat that?" to indicate to your partner that he's said something inappropriate. After all, we cue Nelson at times by saying "heel" or "off" or "leave it" to remind him to be on his good behavior. It's a short message that gets the point across, not a long-winded diatribe on what he did wrong and why we are upset with him. Just as Nelson does, the hope is that your partner will also respond respectfully to your cues.

The next step is to work on restraining yourself from making critical remarks to your mate. Recognize when you are able to exert this type of self-control, and give yourself credit for holding your tongue. You may see an improvement in your relationship simply due to the absence of hurtful and destructive remarks. Next, as we've mentioned previously, concentrating on catching your partner doing something right will help you appreciate his positive traits and behaviors. Finally, be sure to speak up and tell your partner the positives you are now noticing. This entire process will take time to implement, but I have seen many couples succeed in ending the cycle of fault-finding.

Neediness

Nelson is a loving dog, but even he gets weary of being fussed over excessively. He may amble off into another room or go curl up in his bed to have some solitude. Brian, age 35, came in to see me because he had the same impulse to flee as Nelson. Brian's wife of three years, Hilary, was behaving in ways that made him question his feelings for her. Hilary, age 32, seemed to need constant reassurance from Brian about her appearance – Did he think she was pretty? Was she too fat? Were her thighs too jiggly? Was her hair too frizzy?

Not only that, but Hilary said "I love you" to Brian at least five times a day. He was at a loss about how to respond to her questions and frequent assertions of love. The more anxious and insecure Hilary behaved, the more Brian felt himself detaching from her. Of course, his detachment generated more anxiety for Hilary, which then led to even more neediness on her part.

When Hilary came in with Brian for couples counseling, both partners were able to see the cycle in which they had become trapped. Hilary agreed to go into individual therapy to work on her insecurities and to stop asking Brian for reassurance so often. In turn, Brian agreed to make it a point to compliment Hilary occasionally on some aspect of her appearance. Hilary also agreed to cut back on saying "I love you" to Brian. Instead of eliciting pleasure, Hilary's frequent "I love you's" caused Brian to feel resentful and controlled; each time he felt pressured into telling Hilary "I love you, too" to avoid hurting her feelings.

Inexperience and Discomfort

In chapter one, we saw how Rebecca approached her husband Mitch's difficulty with expressing verbal affection.

Rather than continuing to harp on this sore point in their relationship, Rebecca used behavioral shaping techniques to reinforce any slight movement Mitch made either to compliment her or to show appreciation. In the process, their relationship became much more positive and satisfying.

Another couple, Randy and Catherine, came in for therapy to address Catherine's lack of physical and sexual responsiveness. Catherine was raised by a verbally and physically abusive father and a meek, passive mother, somewhat similar to Mitch's family of origin. Catherine was a positive, friendly, and loyal person, but she had great difficulty expressing deep affection for Randy or anyone else. Catherine had been in long-term therapy to address her past abuse and depression. She was currently under the care of a psychiatrist who prescribed antidepressant medication for her.

Catherine was embarrassed and ashamed of her inability to express herself lovingly in her marriage. She felt safer when she could avoid emotional highs and lows. Her childhood had been so volatile that she was naturally hesitant and fearful of re-experiencing hurt and pain. So Catherine channeled her energy into being highly productive and organized in order to avoid examining her feelings.

When both emotional and sexual issues are present, (as they frequently are), I ask couples to suspend consideration of sexual concerns until we address underlying emotional concerns. First we focused on all of the many loving acts Catherine performed for Randy. Even though she worked full-time, Catherine made an effort to provide Randy with delicious home-cooked meals. She helped raise his two daughters from his former marriage, giving of her time and resources generously and lovingly. Upon reflection, Randy realized that Catherine valued his happiness above her own and demonstrated this in countless ways.

Gradually, as Randy stopped taking Catherine's many loving deeds for granted and saw them as acts of caring and sacrifice, he began to treat her differently. He expressed appreciation more often and initiated holding Catherine's hand at times or giving her a hug. Instead of watching and waiting for Catherine to change, Randy tried to lay the groundwork for Catherine to feel safe and accepted in their relationship. He refrained from complaining and criticizing her, and he stopped making demands. Over time, as Randy practiced more tolerance and patience, Catherine was able to risk stepping out of her emotional safety zone. She responded to Randy when he was affectionate, and gradually could respond more fully to him sexually as well.

We know that physical and sexual sharing is important in romantic relationships, but how this sharing is manifested is different for each couple. In this case, Randy was able to honor Catherine's emotional comfort level by not expecting her to take the initiative sexually. This, in turn, meant that Catherine could stop feeling guilty when Randy made demands on her that she wasn't able to fulfill. Randy eventually realized that as long as Catherine was responsive to his overtures, it didn't matter whether or not she initiated contact; they could still have a highly satisfying sexual relationship.

Our inexperience and discomfort can also lead to a troubled relationship with our dog. Dogs need attention, structure, training, affection, and positive reinforcement. We must educate ourselves, both about our dogs and our humans, in order to do the best possible job.

The following is the sad tale of my mother's struggle to raise three different family dogs. My mother would agree that while she was a devoted and caring parent to her three children, she was somewhat delinquent in the dog-parenting department. My mother never had a dog or any interest in dogs, but unfortunately for her, she later had three children who clamored for a dog.

We got Ginger, a furry little mutt, after my brother, sister, and I assured my mother that we were ready to take responsibility for a dog. Poor Ginger never had a chance. I was the oldest, and at nine, I had no idea how to take care of a dog. We not only failed to train him, but we didn't even realize it was necessary. We sometimes gave Ginger affection, but often we handled him with what my mother termed "benign neglect." In those days before leash laws, Ginger ran freely around the neighborhood. When he bit our postman, my mother decided to send Ginger to what she euphemistically referred to as the "farm." For years we envisioned Ginger happily romping around pastures until it finally dawned on us why we never got to go visit Ginger on this particular farm.

A few years later my mother gave into our pleas for a dog once again. Our new dog was an adorable boxer named Sarge. Although we still didn't realize that a dog needed actual training, Sarge was sweet and well-behaved. However, much to our dismay, Sarge was allergic to grass. My mother told people that she gave birth to three children who were allergy-free, while her dog required three trips a week to the veterinarian for allergy shots. Finally, she convinced us that Sarge would be more comfortable living with a family she knew who had a huge expanse of concrete surrounding their house.

The footnote to our sad parting with Sarge is that he became a hero. Two years after he went to live with the new family, Sarge went into the parents' bedroom one night and woke them up. They immediately smelled smoke and got their family and pets out of the house. This was before the era of smoke detectors in homes. Sarge had alerted them to a fire that ultimately destroyed most of their house, and he saved their lives. It seemed like an act of fate that Sarge had gone to live with this family.

So far my mother was two for two. She had not bonded with either dog. But she took care of their basic needs and tolerated them. When my brother was twelve he lobbied for another dog, and, as usual, my mother gave in. (My father worked long hours, so he left these decisions to my mother. He, too, was unfamiliar with dogs and how to take care of them properly). This time, we actually talked to people about what breed would be best for our family and looked up information in several dog books. We selected a little brown, black, and white beagle puppy and named him Godot. My brother chose this name because he claimed he had been "waiting for Godot."

Again, we had dog problems almost immediately, although looking back, they were really due to our ignorance and incompetence. Godot grew from an undisciplined puppy to an incorrigible dog who urinated on my father's galley proofs for the tax book he authored (we all wondered what the publisher must have thought of the yellow-tinged, strange-smelling pages that arrived for that year's tax guide), swiped our steak dinner off the serving cart right in front of us as we sat with our guests waiting to dine, and generally created mayhem wherever he went. After several more incidents, my mother decided Godot needed to go to a home where the people could appreciate him more than we did. She may not have mastered dog-training and discipline, but she certainly perfected the technique of how to tell one's children that the family dog would be better off elsewhere!

The point of relating these dog tales is to not to bash my mother for her lack of dog due diligence. She is the first to acknowledge her limitations in this area. Happily, she has bonded with Nelson and it works out well: My mother doesn't have to assume primary responsibility for him, and Nelson has another human to lavish with love. Rather, the descriptions of my mother's futile attempts to provide us with a family dog illustrate how a dog-owner who is inexperienced and uncomfortable in what is required of her will have difficulty raising a happy, well-behaved dog.

Human couples have the same limitations and requirements. If one or both members of a couple lack knowledge or cannot apply effective communication skills, conflict resolution skills, trust, allegiance, and affection, it is impossible to have a strong, healthy union. On the other hand, when partners bring knowledge and ease to their relationship, they can work together to achieve a happy outcome.

Avoidance or Fear of Intimacy

Some reasons for avoiding or fearing intimacy may include one or more of the following factors: a history of physical or sexual molestation or abuse; current emotional or physical abuse in the relationship; insufficient trust between partners; a strong need to maintain control; medical disability or illness; and mental health issues such as depression, anxiety disorders, eating disorders, and alcoholism.

When one partner has intimacy issues, the entire relationship can be seriously impacted. In the following example, Paul created emotional distance, and even barriers, with his wife, Inez. He didn't show much affection, verbally or physically, and he was often critical and demanding.

Inez and Paul had been married for twenty-two years, with two teenage children, when they came in for couples counseling. When I asked what they wanted to accomplish in our work together, Inez said she wanted a better relationship with Paul. She wanted to feel emotionally closer to him and to stop having so many arguments. In addition, she wanted him to stop looking at pornography on the computer in his study almost every evening. Inez was angry and felt disrespected by Paul's preoccupation with pornography. Paul wanted a better relationship with Inez and a more satisfactory sex life together. Inez and Paul were each looking for many of the same things in their relationship, but they didn't know how to get past the barriers they had established with each other.

Paul grew up in a family where there was little communication and affection. His parents both worked long hours, and as soon as they were old enough, Paul and his three siblings were left to fend for themselves after school and in the evenings. On weekends, Paul's family went their separate ways. Paul learned at an early age not to expect much from others.

Inez, on the other hand, came from a loving and supportive family where she received a great deal of affection and attention. Part of her initial attraction to Paul was based on her compassion for him because of his lonely childhood. Inez felt blessed because of her happy upbringing, and she wanted to give Paul the affection and love he had been lacking.

In working with this couple, it soon became apparent that Paul had great difficulty accepting affection and caring from Inez. He wasn't used to receiving affection and it made him uncomfortable. Subconsciously, it also brought up how unhappy, helpless, and resentful he felt as a child – feelings he didn't want to re-experience. Although he wasn't aware of why he was doing it, Paul pushed Inez away emotionally in many different ways. He criticized her often, especially about sensitive areas such as her weight and her choice of friends. Paul frequently complained to Inez about her lack of receptivity in their sexual relationship, and at the same time, he didn't hide the fact from her that he frequently viewed computer porn. In his words and actions, Paul was sending a message that he considered Inez inadequate in many ways.

How was Paul's behavior going to accomplish what he said he wanted – greater intimacy with Inez, both emotionally and physically? Obviously, it wasn't. Inez had distanced herself from Paul emotionally in order to protect herself, and was no longer very accessible to him. If I were to scold Nelson several times a day and rarely touched him, what kind of bond would we have? Dogs give us unconditional love under the right circumstances, but even they don't fully respond to us if we don't treat them well.

Despite these problems, Paul and Inez got along well when situations didn't involve highly personal matters. They both worked in the same field as realtors, and they shared many similar interests and values. They agreed on most parenting issues and both were involved, caring parents.

After many therapy sessions, Paul began to understand some of the issues underlying his behavior in the relationship, and he worked on improving his treatment of Inez. Paul looked at how viewing pornography when his wife was in the next room not only distanced him from her emotionally, but also depersonalized their sexual relationship. It took some time since this behavior had become habitual, but eventually Paul was able to stop.

Inez would only be able to establish trust if Paul could show her that he was willing to discard his tendency to blame and criticize, even during periods of conflict. Although Inez was deeply hurt by Paul, she was willing to give him a chance to show her how much he loved her and wanted to continue being with her. Paul went into individual therapy to deal more thoroughly with his painful childhood and its effects on him. Paul and Inez continued their work together in couples therapy until they were on a positive track and were able to give and receive the love and affection they both desired.

Take a personal inventory of what may be interfering with your own ability to express affection, verbally or physically, with your partner. You may need to seek individual therapy if you have issues that are too difficult to resolve on your own, especially if you have a history of abuse or self-destructive behavior. It may take some hard work along the way, but allowing yourself to give and receive affection will ultimately bring you the fulfillment you deserve.

9

Fifi, No Other Dog Can Ever Take Your Place
Encourage Loyalty and Faithfulness

*"The fidelity of a dog is a precious gift demanding no
less binding moral responsibilities than the friendship
of a human being. The bond with a true dog is as
lasting as the ties of this earth can ever be."*
—Konrad Lorenz

WHEN FIFI LIES ON HER BACK and exposes her tummy for
a belly rub, she is displaying total trust in her human. This
position is not a natural one for any animal unless there is a
sense of absolute safety in the environment.

Fifi shows complete trust in you in many other ways as
well. She follows your commands to come or stay without
hesitation (well, most of the time anyway). When she is alone
at home, she trusts that her human will return to take care
of her. She allows you to brush her, cut her nails, pick out
burrs, and clean her ears and eyes, even if it is uncomfortable
or sometimes painful for her.

Dogs are loyal and faithful by nature, but we need to
demonstrate reliability for them to continue to trust us. If we
offer frequent praise, attention, affection, and rewards, Fifi

will respond to us with all of her being. But if we neglect Fifi or are cruel to her, she will learn not to count on us and may withdraw or develop aggressive behavior in response.

Similarly, when we offer frequent praise, attention, affection, and rewards to our human partner, we increase the likelihood of receiving loyalty and faithfulness in return. But if we ignore or neglect our partner's needs, the relationship will invariably suffer. Just like Fifi, our partner will learn not to fully trust us. He may withdraw or become angry or even hostile. He may even turn to someone else to attempt to fulfill his needs.

We have looked at the importance of showing affection and appreciation to our partner. Now let's explore how we can give our partner the kind of care that is essential for a close, lasting relationship.

Actively share interest in each other's work and activities

One of my closest friends has been happily married for many decades. I was there at the beginning when Linda and Alan met, and was later a bridesmaid in their wedding. Through the years I have watched how well they support each other in every way possible. They help each other with work projects despite being in very different kinds of careers. They pitch in together to help their family and friends, and they talk and laugh often.

But there is one special thing that stands out in their relationship. Alan is a self-described golf fanatic and plays every chance he gets. Linda doesn't play golf, but nonetheless, she manages to actively share this interest with Alan. Frequently Linda accompanies Alan while he plays golf, riding in the golf cart and enjoying the scenery and Alan's company. Sometimes she brings a good book, but often she just takes pleasure in the experience. Linda talks with Alan about his golf scores, shots, and frustrations, and she is his biggest fan when he has a successful game. Sharing Alan's favorite activity brings them closer.

This doesn't mean that it is necessary to participate in all of your partner's activities. Linda and Alan spend time on their own individual pursuits as well. Having separate interests is important and can help make your relationship more stimulating. But when possible, even if you are not actually scuba-diving, playing bridge, or running races, you can still be an active part of your partner's experiences.

You take Fifi to the dog park and other places that she is interested in, purely so that she can enjoy herself. You share her pleasure when she is participating in her favorite activities, even if it means you stand around and watch her play. And sometimes you look for places to take her that you will also enjoy, such as on a hike or to the beach. Just as you do with Fifi, it helps to give your partner the treat of sharing experiences with one another as often as possible.

Find common interests to share

We have already discussed the importance of sharing some interests and activities together. Many couples reach a point at some time in their relationship when they realize that their lives are heading in separate directions. If you each are devoting much more time to your own activities, friends, and interests than to one another, it is time to establish a better balance in your relationship. Finding one or two common interests to pursue together is vital. These activities may change from time to time, of course, but the important thing is to maintain a healthy level of involvement with each other. Exploring new interests together can add excitement, fun, and a greater sense of connection for a couple.

Actively share interest in each other's thoughts and feelings

One couple I worked with found a way to ensure they would check in with each other to share thoughts and feelings. Peter and Carrie's lives were extremely hectic. They felt like business partners instead of spouses much of the time, with most conversations rushed and limited to details about meals, home repairs, carpools and kids. Peter and Carrie decided to commit to a date night together one night a week. They hired a high school student for a few hours every Thursday night. Occasionally they went to a movie or a concert, but usually they tried to make time for conversation with each other. On these date nights, they prohibited talk about their three children or practical concerns about the house, the yard, the car, etc. Instead they tried to use this time to connect emotionally with each other – to share their thoughts and feelings and to laugh and enjoy each other's company.

How often do we hear someone try to justify an extramarital affair by saying "My husband/wife just doesn't understand me?" Or, "My husband/wife doesn't give me what I need?" Relationships in which both partners feel closely connected emotionally and physically have a better chance of avoiding betrayal and disloyalty.

Earlier we discussed the importance of being an active listener with your partner so that you enjoy spending time together. Active listening also helps promote closeness and loyalty in a relationship. Let's look again at how this concept can make a difference. For example, in order to show your partner you are interested in what she says, you must do more than nod your head or say, "I see." When Fifi performs a trick for you, do you just smile slightly or do you enthusiastically say "good dog?" In your response to your partner, if you can try to match the emotions behind her words, you will be doing a good job as an active listener.

When Meg tells her boyfriend, Phil, "I'm really sad I can't afford to visit my sister more often." she is looking for a supportive and understanding reaction from him. If Phil's response is, "Yeah" or "Uh-huh," he is not showing Meg he grasps the extent of her feelings. He is not acknowledging her sadness. An example of a response that would show understanding and support would be, "That's hard for you. I know you miss her."

Even if Phil takes the stereotypically male tactic of trying to fix the situation and says, "Then why don't you invite her to come stay with us?" he's at least putting more energy and content into his response. He's more closely matching the mood behind Meg's statement. A simple "yeah" or "uh-huh" is almost a brush-off when someone is trying to communicate a heartfelt emotion. They may be adequate responses for a less emotional statement, such as "I wish it were Friday," or "I'm tired of eating fish." Try to match the seriousness and importance of your partner's message with a corresponding response. After all, when Fifi approaches you enthusiastically to have her belly scratched, she appreciates a matching response from you, and not just a brief, lack-luster belly rub.

With the onslaught of media and electronic devices in our homes, some couples get into the habit of only partially listening to one another. His eye may be on the televised football game while she may be texting their daughter or listening to her iPod. Fifi wants our full attention and so does our partner. Take a tip from Fifi if you aren't receiving the attention you want. Fifi politely insists on making full contact. She may stand directly in front of us, or rub up against us, or jump up on our lap. She doesn't go off to mope with hurt feelings. She sticks with her intent of communicating with us.

Demonstrate Understanding with your Words and Actions

It's not enough to just tell our partner that we understand; we need to show him. If Sheila tells Rod that her back hurts, it's very nice if he expresses sympathy. But it is also important for Rod to *show* his sympathy by voluntarily carrying the groceries, laundry basket, and any heavy items, and by asking Sheila how her back feels and what he can do to help her. Similarly, if Rod comes home from work saying that he's feeling tired and discouraged, Sheila can not only show empathy, but she can also offer to give him a massage, or suggest that he sit and relax while she takes over the dinner and childcare chores for the evening.

On a deeper level, we all want to feel understood and accepted by our loved ones. Understanding implies acceptance, at least to some extent. For example, when Rod calls in sick to work when he isn't really ill, if Sheila expresses understanding she is also indicating a certain level of acceptance. She tries to see the situation from Rod's point of view and not just her own, and she tries not to judge.

And Sheila would like to feel understood and accepted when she tells Rod how upset she is that their neighbors' dog barks incessantly. After all, not all dogs are as well-behaved as Fifi. She doesn't want Rod to point out reasons why she shouldn't feel the way she does – "Dogs will tend to bark, you're being overly sensitive, you need to calm down." Sheila would like Rod to show he understands why she's upset and then ask if she wants his help in figuring out a possible solution.

If Sheila shares her feelings about having a difficult time around the Christmas holidays because they bring up painful memories, Rod can encourage her to talk more about these feelings. Then he can find ways to demonstrate his understanding. He can ask Sheila what would help her and then automatically implement her wishes as much as possible during the holidays. Perhaps it helps Sheila to spend the holidays in a different setting or to commemorate them much differently than she did while growing up. She won't have to explain her moods and feelings every year because Rod will remember and will help take care of her in this way.

Take Your Partner's Side

If Rod comes home from work steaming about how unfair his boss is, Sheila needs to let Rod know immediately that she sympathizes with him and sees his point of view. Rod's most immediate need is to feel understood and validated. Even if Rod is a chronic complainer or if Sheila suspects the boss has a point, the best thing she can do initially is to express solidarity with Rod. If Sheila reacts skeptically, it will not make a difference in Rod's perceptions or reactions at the time; he will simply feel letdown and possibly alienated from Sheila because she isn't on his side. Later, after Rod has calmed down, Sheila can ask Rod if he wants to talk more about what happened. He may then be able to gain more insight into the situation and perhaps view it differently.

Sheila is not being a hypocrite by immediately showing Rod support. Rather, she is demonstrating that he is the most important person to her and that his feelings matter. In other words, she is showing him that "she has his back." This display of loyalty is important for the relationship to thrive.

Similarly, Rod needs to take Sheila's side with others. If Rod's mother finds fault with Sheila's tendency to be disorganized, Rod needs to avoid agreeing with her. If his buddies complain that Sheila is too controlling because she sometimes objects to their frequent fishing trips, Rod needs to refrain from joining in to criticize her.

Each partner needs to be especially careful not to disagree or find fault with the other around their children. I see many couples whose relationships have deteriorated because one or both take the other to task in front of their children. It certainly is unhealthy for the children to witness and only produces hurt, resentment, and anger between partners.

Speak Highly of Your Partner to Others

We all need to vent and complain at times about those who are close to us. We even complain about Fifi if she wakes us up too often at night or if she digs in the yard. But on whole, it is better to speak about our partner in a positive way with others. And if we can do this while he is present, this is icing on the cake. Words spoken in a public forum often have an even higher impact than those we say privately. Allow your partner to bask in the compliments and supportive words you use as you mention him to others. Fifi's ears certainly perk up when we tell others what a good dog she is. We need to do this for our partner too.

Share a sense of humor and use it often

We tend to most enjoy being with people who make us feel good about ourselves when we are with them. We want to feel interesting and fun, and that our partner brings out the best in us. It is natural to gravitate to those who help us accentuate our most positive traits.

Relationships where each partner uses humor and appreciates the other's sense of humor have a distinct advantage. There is an unspoken bond when each person can depend on the other to enhance the relationship in this way. Humor can help diffuse difficult situations ("Maybe we need to make the garage larger so you won't have to sideswipe the car on the way in."), it can promote intimacy, and it can provide fun and entertainment in a relationship.

Let your partner know frequently how much you appreciate his sense of humor. Humor is individualistic and creative; by telling him you value this trait you are also letting him know you appreciate him.

Being Faithful Involves Full Disclosure

It is easier for one who feels accepted and loved in a relationship to come clean about bad habits or personal deficiencies. But even if one partner isn't feeling fully valued by the other, it is still an issue of integrity to disclose an event or relationship with potential impact on one's partner. As I constantly witness in my therapy practice, past or present problems inevitably come to light. It is far better to voluntarily disclose information to a loved one than to have her stumble upon a hidden bank account or an illicit relationship. How one handles a personal failing makes a big difference in whether or not a relationship can survive a breakdown of trust.

One couple I saw had been married for six years, with two children ages one and three. They came in because Malcolm had just discovered that Monique was having an affair with a mutual acquaintance from their gym. He was devastated, and although he thought there was not much hope, Malcolm wanted to see if the relationship could be salvaged.

Unfortunately for Malcolm, Monique was not very contrite. She blamed Malcolm for much of their unhappy marriage, and she felt somewhat justified in turning to another man. We worked together for a few months until it became clear that Monique was unwilling to accept responsibility for her behavior. She continued to portray herself as the victim in the marriage, and she refused to end the relationship with the other man. This marriage was doomed.

In contrast, Miguel had been having an affair with a woman in his office for several months. When his wife, Rita, confronted him with evidence she had gathered, Miguel readily admitted his mistake. He begged Rita, his wife of twenty-three years, for the chance to prove to her that he could reform. He said he didn't like or respect himself and that Rita deserved much better. Because Miguel acknowledged responsibility for his actions, Rita was willing to try to repair the relationship. This couple is still working hard in marriage counseling, and their relationship has a good prognosis.

Handle conflict respectfully and fairly

All couples experience conflict in their relationship from time to time. Many issues will never be completely resolved. But *how* couples handle conflict is what determines whether or not they can respect each other and be happy together. Dr. John Gottman refers to the Four Horsemen of the Apocalypse that interfere with good communication and, according to his research, can signify a destructive relationship: criticism, contempt, defensiveness, and stonewalling.

Contempt goes beyond criticism and usually involves a disparaging tone of voice and facial expression, as well as harsh words of disgust. Defensiveness prevents a discussion or argument from proceeding forward; it keeps the parties bogged down in a "he said, she said" verbal exchange as each one defends his or her position. When a person stonewalls, he refuses to participate in a conversation and either withdraws, ignores, or refuses to talk.

Entire books are devoted to how to fight fairly, but here are the most important points to remember:

*Avoid insulting, labeling, cursing, threatening, and accusing. These behaviors are indications of verbal abusiveness if employed often and cruelly. At the least, they sabotage any effort to establish cooperative communication with one's partner. The recipient will become angry, defensive, may stonewall, and ultimately will feel alienated.

*Avoid pounding, throwing items, pointing fingers in a partner's face, a menacing stance, and any act of physical violence. These behaviors clearly indicate a huge loss of control and will be extremely destructive for the relationship.

*Don't use confidences, worries, or intimate details your partner has shared with you as weapons in an argument. Not only will your partner become hurt and enraged, but he will lose trust and will stop confiding in you.

*Do use "I" messages to avoid blaming and attacking. Tell your partner how you feel, what is causing you to feel this way, and what you would like her to do or to say differently that will help. For example, "I'm frustrated about not being on time for social occasions. I'm always ready to go and then need to wait for you. I would like it if you could be ready to leave at the time we have agreed upon. Are you willing to help me with this problem?"

*Listen to your partner without interrupting. Try not to be thinking of what you are going to say next, and instead concentrate on what your partner is saying.

*Then clarify what your partner said. Repeat back what you heard and how you interpret what was said. Often, we rush in to argue when we haven't listened fully and accurately to what our partner was trying to communicate.

*Try to look beyond the content of the argument to find possible resolutions. Instead of getting bogged down in a frequent argument over who isn't doing enough to help with the house or the children, figure out what would help the situation. Make suggestions and use a problem-solving approach.

*Timing is important. Don't start or continue arguments when one or both partners are tired, hungry, emotionally exhausted, or are already provoked. Wait for a good time to bring up an important issue.

*Keep in mind all of the traits you value in your partner so that your anger doesn't throw you off track. Try to have some perspective, even in the midst of an argument. Ask yourself how you would deal with a friend if you were in the same situation. Would you be calmer and more patient? Take a time-out or cooling off period if you need it. It is fine to ask your partner to postpone a discussion as long as you establish a new time that is mutually agreeable.

*Don't bring up past grievances. No one likes to be reminded of past mistakes or hurtful experiences. Your partner will likely react negatively, and you will fail to keep your discussion on a positive, solution-oriented track. Stick to current dissatisfactions only.

*If you are still affected by past issues, see a therapist. Many people have difficulty dealing with a betrayal of trust in a relationship. If your partner had an affair or did something else that caused you enormous pain, it will take a lot of time to heal and to see if it is possible to surmount this obstacle to your relationship. Constant focus on difficult issues puts a relationship into a downward spiral. Most couples aren't equipped to deal with all of the consequences by themselves, so intervention is extremely important. In the case of an affair, it is beneficial for each partner to have some individual therapy and for the couple to seek couples counseling.

Try Hard to Forgive

One of the things we like best about our dogs is that they easily forgive us for our mistakes. If we forget to feed Fifi a meal or fail to take her on her daily walk, she will be as loving as usual with us. Of course, dogs don't comprehend exactly what happened and whose fault it is, but the point here is that Fifi does not hold a grudge against us when things go wrong or don't happen. She simply loves us unconditionally.

Humans are definitely more complicated, but we can learn from Fifi's example. There is a reason why dogs are easily pleased and content. They accept all of the good things we do for them, and they don't harbor resentment if we fail them in some way. This reasoning doesn't apply, of course, if we are cruel or mistreat Fifi. Abuse, in both human and canine relationships, will inevitably lead to a breakdown in trust and loyalty.

Cesar Millan, the " Dog Whisperer," a popular expert on dog-training, points out the importance of not holding grudges. He says, "There's a remarkable lack of conflict in dog packs. That's because members resolve the situation when disagreements arise, then move on... Holding onto negative feelings tends to make them multiply and prevents us from moving forward."

Forgiveness for humans is not as automatic as it is for dogs, but it is still attainable. It helps if your partner shows you in every way possible that he has remorse for the hurt he has caused you. If he is not truly repentant, it is harder to move beyond the breach of trust, and the relationship will suffer and may not survive.

Forgiveness is not just important for the health of the relationship. It is also important for the health of the individuals, especially if you are the betrayed party. Holding onto anger and hurt causes unhappiness and distress, and can isolate you from others who may grow weary of hearing your constant litany of grievances.

In addition, your immune system may suffer from increased cortisol, sometimes referred to as the "stress hormone." As we have previously noted, cortisol is secreted by the adrenal glands in higher levels during the body's response to stress. Some adverse affects can include lowered immunity, increased inflammatory responses, higher blood pressure, and increased abdominal fat which contributes to heart attacks and strokes.

So, take a hint from Fifi who lives a very happy existence. Give your partner your attention, interest, understanding, and acceptance. Maintain a sense of humor in your relationship. Share your innermost thoughts and feelings with your partner and encourage him to reciprocate. Try hard to release grudges and find forgiveness. Even though we know that Fifi is *really* your best friend, try hard to make your partner your best human friend!

10

Nelson, Would You Like Some Gravy with Your Steak?

Encourage a Healthy Lifestyle

"He is your friend, your partner, your defender, your
dog. You are his life, his love, his leader. He will be
yours, faithful and true. To the last beat of his heart.
You owe it to him to be worthy of such devotion."
—Anonymous

WE PUT EFFORT INTO ENSURING OUR dog gets enough food, exercise, and play time. Sometimes, we may even go overboard. There are dog owners who will only feed Fifi homemade dog food containing the purest ingredients. There are dog owners who pay for their dogs to go to expensive daily play groups. In a 2009 survey conducted by the American Kennel Club to find out how the downturn in the economy was affecting dog care, seventy-eight percent of the respondents said they would cancel a teeth-whitening appointment of their own in order to pay for their dog's annual teeth cleanings. And sixty-five percent of the respondents said they would eat instant noodles to be able to continue to afford high quality food for their dogs.

But do we put as much effort and sacrifice into the day-to-day health and maintenance of our partners and ourselves? We may complain that our spouse is working long hours or worry that he is not eating well or getting enough rest or exercise, but do we take an active role in making sure he is leading a healthy lifestyle? And are we vigilant about our own dietary and exercise habits? We may pamper our dogs with lavender spa packs, special massages, pawdicures (believe it or not!), aromatherapy products such as fur butter, and much more. But after we lavish so much attention on our dog, do we also spend time pampering our partner and ourselves?

According to books on the principles of dog training, a consistent routine is important. The routine calls for proper nutrition (not overfeeding), sufficient exercise, comfortable sleep, stimulation and play with toys, contact with other dogs when possible, and human affection and interaction. Many dogs need a job to perform in order to be truly fulfilled. They may train to be therapy dogs and visit senior residences, or listen to children read to them in libraries. Or they may enjoy following commands, performing tricks, and doing chores. (Nelson and I seem to have reached an impasse in his training. I recently tried to teach him to crawl, and after much coaxing he now lies down and limply places one paw out in front of his body). Time management is also important. There needs to be time for play, for socialization, for grooming needs, for work, and for being alone.

Social skills are essential – learning to share, take turns, respect limits, pay attention, and cooperate. These ingredients help to produce a happy, fulfilled dog. Nelson is the most sociable dog we've ever had. Before Nelson we had a beloved chow named Chelsey. She was wonderful, but she had no interest in socializing with anyone out of her pack, our immediate family. Nelson, however, sometimes receives more social invites than we do. He is naturally agreeable and gets along well because he doesn't care about being the alpha dog. He has highly developed social skills that make him a popular guy in the neighborhood.

A healthy lifestyle for humans also means finding a good balance between work, play, relationships and socializing, hobbies and interests, exercise, sleep, and relaxation. If one or more of these areas becomes excessive, an imbalance may develop that can threaten a relationship.

Corinne came for therapy because she was worried and discouraged. Her husband of eighteen years, Ryan, was spending more and more time on his BlackBerry. During the past two years he took it everywhere, and it seemed to Corinne that Ryan was constantly on call for his job. She noticed that he even got up regularly in the middle of the night to check his messages. When Ryan went to their son's hockey game, he spent more time emailing, talking, and texting than he did watching their son play. Even during social occasions, such as dinners and weddings, Ryan ducked out frequently to check his messages.

Corinne worried at first that Ryan was having an affair, but this was not the case. He had a responsible position in his company, and he felt compelled to respond immediately whenever he was contacted. While this was not part of Ryan's job description, he didn't feel comfortable unless he was in constant communication. Ryan's behavior became more and more compulsive until it reached the point where Corinne felt ignored and discounted.

Ryan refused to come in for couples counseling, so instead Corinne worked alone on ways to salvage her marriage. We looked at how her frequent complaints and accusations weren't accomplishing her goal of having Ryan more present in the relationship. She had tried busying herself with lots of activities so that Ryan would experience how it felt to be ignored. Nothing seemed to work.

Our approach was nothing elaborate. It simply called for Corinne to invite Ryan out to dinner with her one night for a heart-to-heart conversation. She let him know how sad and lonely she was in their marriage and how his lack of attention caused her to feel unloved and unworthy. She asked him if he still loved her, and he said he did. She basically put herself at his mercy and asked him if he was willing to help. Ryan agreed to make a change. He said he would stop taking his BlackBerry out when he was socializing or attending their son's activities, and that he would limit its use at home as well.

The reason Corinne's approach worked this time is that she explained specifically how Ryan's behavior affected her. She spoke from a personal perspective, and didn't blame, attack, complain, or threaten as she had in the past. As a result, Ryan was less defensive and was finally able to hear how damaging his BlackBerry addiction was, both to Corinne's self-worth and to their relationship.

If Nelson had a bad habit, such as barking too much or being aggressive with other dogs, we would seek help from various resources — online sites, books, a trainer, or other dog-owners. Nelson is a wonderful dog so far, but we have had dogs in the past where we've needed to consult experts for help with training and discipline. We need to recognize when to seek consultation for ourselves and our humans as well. The following case illustrates how important it is to seek help when there are signs of unhealthy, compulsive behavior.

Even though we all know that exercise has many benefits and is important to incorporate into our everyday lives, too much of a good thing can become a problem. Daria was a twenty-eight year old real estate agent who lived with her boyfriend of two years, Luis. She came in for help with her addiction to exercise. Daria had always been in good physical shape, but as she got older she became more and more hooked on how working out made her feel. She felt strong, healthy, in control, and energetic. Gradually, she began to structure her days around exercising, and she went to the gym twice a day for ninety-minute workouts. If she missed even one day of exercise, Daria became irritable, anxious, and extremely critical of herself; she would tell herself she was lazy, fat, and ugly. As time went on, Daria became increasingly dissatisfied with herself since no amount of exercise felt sufficient to her.

In therapy, Daria began the process of confronting her fears. She had never felt "good enough" in her relationships with men. Daria had a huge fear of rejection, and therefore she didn't risk getting too close to anyone. With the combination of her job and her gym habit, Daria didn't make much time for her boyfriend and their relationship. It was as if she already had one foot out the door. Because Daria felt inadequate in so many ways, having a toned, trim body helped give her the confidence she lacked. But gradually Daria became addicted to the good feelings she derived from exercising, and she increasingly needed more and more of this "drug" to feel okay.

Daria spent over two years in therapy. After she understood how her difficult past experiences with her family and former relationships helped shape her, literally and figuratively, she was able to work toward a better balance in her life.

Excessive exercise was a poor substitute for the self-esteem and confidence in herself that Daria needed.

Many people in our society suffer from other types of excess, namely food, alcohol, and drugs. When an individual is affected, so are at least four to six other people in his life. It is true that no one can be helped unless he is receptive to making a change. There are usually many underlying contributing factors to these kinds of addictions. Since food, alcohol, and drug addiction are inevitably complex issues, some kind of intervention is usually the only effective treatment. Intervention can be in the form of organizations such as Alcoholics Anonymous or Overeaters Anonymous, an inpatient or outpatient treatment program, or individual or group therapy. Treatment often must address a combination of medical, emotional, behavioral, and spiritual issues.

Just as we vigilantly try to meet Fifi's needs and keep her healthy, so must we be attentive to the needs of our partner. There are many thriving, well-treated pooches living amidst very unhealthy humans. If your partner is not in the frame of mind to help himself, either because of denial, depression, or resistance, you can do your best to motivate him to change. Of course, no one wants to be nagged. But there are ways to encourage him without arousing anger and resentment.

Research that shows that people tend to copy habits of those close to them, such as smoking, overeating, and lack of exercise. You can be a good role-model for your mate by seeing your doctor and dentist regularly, and by practicing healthy habits. You can limit the kinds of foods that you bring into the house, and you can serve appropriate portions when you are the one preparing a meal. You don't tempt Fifi with large portions of greasy food, (well … maybe a special supplement to her dog food here and there), so you know it is important not to tempt your partner with large, unhealthy portions. And just as you wouldn't be cruel and sit right in front of Fifi slowly devouring a juicy steak as she watches, you need to eat your own treats out of sight of your partner if he is overweight.

If you are in good physical shape with moderate eating and drinking behavior, you will be demonstrating alternatives for him, without even saying a word. Few people over the age of two respond well to being told what to do or to being criticized, so think of other ways to encourage him to be healthier. Fortunately you have Fifi who loves to walk and run and play. Try to include your partner in this activity with you and Fifi, or ask him to take over for you at times when you are busy. Think of activities that you can do together that will require exercise, such as hiking or kayaking. Enlist family and friends to join in active pursuits with you. Choose wisely when dining out, since restaurant meals can be full of hidden fats and calories. And try to limit passive activities, such as watching television or sitting at the computer, as much as possible.

Chronic, excessive alcohol consumption, drug addiction, and life-threatening obesity are more serious issues. Sadly, many individuals only decide to take steps to overcome these addictions after they hit bottom. A medical emergency, a job termination, or the loss of a driver's license can finally push them into action. You will need a great deal of support if you are still in the relationship; many addicts push away those close to them with behavior that is either angry and defiant or passive, shut down, and depressed.

Organizations such as Al-Anon, community support groups, and/or therapy can help you. You can also enlist your partner's doctor to be an active advocate for his health. Sometimes an objective professional expert can make some headway. Encourage your partner to talk to his doctor and also to a mental health professional. Try to phrase this request in a loving, caring way. For example, you love him and you will be able to worry less if he talks to someone. Sometimes, though, we are powerless to help another person change, even if it is in his best interest. You will ultimately need to do what is right for yourself and for your family.

Another obstacle to achieving a healthy lifestyle is stress. Modern life is full of complexities and stressors. As we've already mentioned, too much stress can cause serious physiological changes in our bodies. Stress can lead to high blood pressure, increased blood glucose levels, ulcers, sleep disturbances, increased cholesterol, and many other problems. And some of these symptoms can produce serious consequences such as a heart attack, stroke, or diabetes.

Complicated lifestyles often put pressure on relationships and add to stress levels. Dogs don't need to surround themselves with luxury to be content. Give Nelson a bowl of water, some food, a large spot for his gangly body to spread out, and some companionship, and he's a happy puppy. Of course, he does love it if he gets to have a special treat or if he can splash in a river or lake, but he can be content with very little. And because Nelson lives a simple, uncomplicated lifestyle, he is not at all stressed. Except for the occasions when he sees our suitcases by the front door, he is the picture of doggy bliss.

If your life is too stressful, look for ways to simplify. Slow the pace, de-clutter, and limit expenditures and decisions. Surround yourself with others who offer a calming influence. If you must work long hours, be sure to take good care of yourself during your free time. Balance is important. Just like Fifi, you need enough rest, play, exercise, stimulation, and social interaction, along with good nutrition and a calm environment. Work together with your partner to help reduce stress in your lives. Fifi gets dog tired of seeing her humans endlessly chase their tails without achieving satisfaction. After all, she needs you to be physically and emotionally healthy so you can give her the excellent care she deserves.

Conclusion

I wrote this book because I was struck by the irony of how we treat our dogs so well, while we often overlook our relationships with our partners. We have the potential to improve this situation so that we at least treat our partners as well as our dogs. (We already know that your relationship with Fifi is just fine, just like Nelson's and mine). I hope this book has provided you with motivation and tools for improving your human relationship. Since we are more complex beings than our dogs, our human relationships naturally require much more thought and effort. But we can take away many lessons from the way we interact with our lovable canine companions and apply them to our partners.

Treating your partner like a dog means applying the same patience, loyalty, and tenacity to your human relationship that you devote to your dog. It means that if you aren't getting along well enough with your partner, you will take time to figure out possible steps and solutions. The challenge is to take a rational problem-solving approach instead of letting your emotions dominate. If Fifi keeps pulling on her leash when you walk her, you don't yell at her and yank her, day after day, in a futile effort to get her to change. Instead, you think of strategies to change her behavior, and you try to keep your emotions in check.

We often hear the expression "relationships take work." It is important to ask ourselves if we routinely *do* the necessary work. If we don't, we may not be as happy and fulfilled in our relationships as we would like. Or, worse, our relationships may become fractured and ultimately dissolve.

Even when serious issues exist, it is often possible to resolve them with professional help. In many instances, trust can be restored, infidelity issues can be repaired, and communication can be greatly improved. When both partners are willing to put in the necessary time and effort, anything is possible.

Sometimes I see discouraged couples who come in to work on dissolving their relationship amicably, usually for the sake of their children. I honestly believe that these same couples wouldn't give up as easily on their family dog. If they had a dog with huge challenges, they would most likely consult specialists and learn more about how to train, control, and socialize him. Very few dog-owners relinquish their dogs because of incompatibility. But sadly, many humans in relationships give up because of "irreconcilable differences."

My hope is that you experience as much joy with your mate as you do with Fifi. Nelson and Fifi live wonderful lives with their loved ones. Why shouldn't you and your partner be able to do the same?

Appendix

Resources for Training Humans:

Chuong-Kim, Margaret. *The Health Benefits of Physical Touch*, http://www.drbenkim.com, 2005.

Coleman, Joshua. *The Marriage Makeover: Finding Happiness in Imperfect Harmony.* New York, NY: St. Martin's Press, 2003.

Davis, Jeanie Lerche. *What's So Great About Kissing?* http://www.medicinenet.com, 2001.

Gottman, John and Nan Silver. The Seven Principles for Making Marriage Work. London, England: Orion Books, 1999.

Gray, John., Ph.D. *What Your Mother Couldn't Tell You and Your Father Didn't Know.* New York, NY: HarperCollins, 1994.

Haltzman, Scott, M.D. with Theresa Foy DiGeronimo. *The Secrets of Happily Married Men.* San Francisco, CA: Jossey-Bass, 2006.

Haltzman, Scott, M.D. and Theresa Foy DiGeronimo. *The Secrets of Happily Married Women.* San Francisco, CA: Jossey-Bass, 2008.

Love, Patricia., Ed.D. and Stosny, Steven, Ph.D. *How to Improve Your Marriage Without Talking About It: Finding Love Beyond Words.* New York, NY: Broadway Books, 2007.

Madanes, Chloe. *Strategic Family Therapy*. San Francisco, CA: Jossey-Bass, Inc., 1981.

Markman, Howard J., Scott M. Stanley, and Susan L. Blumberg. *Fighting for Your Marriage: A Deluxe Revised Edition of the Classic Best-seller for Enhancing Marriage and Preventing Divorce*. Jossey-Bass, 2010.

National Center for Health Statistics, 2003, Hyattsville, Maryland.

Sanford, Keith. *Communication during Marital Conflict: When Couples Alter their Appraisal, They Change their Behavior*. Journal of Family Psychology, 2006, 256265.

Tannen, Deborah., Ph.D. *You Just Don't Understand: Men and Women in Conversation*. New York, NY: Ballantine Books, 1990.

Wile, Daniel B. *After the Honeymoon: How Conflict Can Improve Your Relationship*. Daniel Wile, 2008.

Resources for Training Dogs:

Coren, Stanley, Ph.D. *In Tough Economic Times People Will Make Sacrifices for their Dog's Happiness*, http://www.psychologytoday.com, 2009.

Dennison, Pamela. *Positive Dog Training*. New York, NY: Penguin Group, 2005.

Millan, Cesar with Melissa Jo Peltier. *Cesar's Way: The Natural, Everyday Guide to Understanding and Correcting Common Dog Problems*. New York, NY: Three Rivers Press, 2006.

Miller, Pat. *The Power of Positive Dog Training*. New York, NY: Howell Book House, 2001.

Tess of Helena. *Training People: How to Bring Out the Best in Your Human*. San Francisco, CA: Chronicle Books, 2007.

The Monks of New Skete. *How To Be Your Dog's Best Friend.* Boston, MA: Little, Brown, and Company, 2002.

The Monks of New Skete. *The Art of Raising a Puppy.* Boston, MA: Little, Brown, and Company, 1991.

Thomas, Elizabeth Marshall. *The Hidden Life of Dogs.* New York, NY: Houghton Mifflin Company, 1993.

U.S. Pet Ownership and Demographics Sourcebook, 2002.

Volhard, Jack and Wendy. *Dog Training for Dummies.* Hoboken, NJ: Wiley Publishing, Inc., 2005.

Whiting, Sam. *Even in Recession, Furry Friends Come First,* San Francisco Chronicle Newpaper, December 15, 2008.

Woodhouse, Barbara. *No Bad Dogs the Woodhouse Way.* New York, NY: Summit Books, 1982.

Acknowledgments

Thanks to my literary agent, Joanne Brownstein, for your help and for your faith in this book. Thanks to Barry Hunau for drawing delightful cartoons, and to Steve Zanki for the cover photo.

Thanks to Vic Ryerson for your invaluable assistance, humor, and loving support. Thanks to Laurel Ryerson and Jennifer Ryerson for your creative contributions and for being such blessings in my life. Thanks to my mother, Marjorie C. Strasburger, for your legacy of compassion, strength, laughter, and love.

Thanks to Susan Strasburger, Dr. Victor Strasburger, and Andrea Pfeiffer for your constant support for me and my projects through the years. And much appreciation goes to my friends and other family members for your helpful ideas, encouragement, and loving presence in my life.

Without the couples I have seen in my therapy practice, I couldn't have written this book. Without my sweet dog, Nelson, and all the dogs I have loved, I couldn't have conceived this book. And without my very dear husband, Vic, I wouldn't have a partner to practice treating like a dog.

About the Author

Margie Ryerson, M.S., MFT, is a licensed marriage and family therapist in the San Francisco Bay Area. She has worked with hundreds of couples in her therapy practice and has conducted workshops for couples through hospital and community programs. She is also the author of *Appetite for Life: Inspiring Stories of Recovery from Anorexia, Bulimia, and Compulsive Overeating*. She lives with her husband and dog and has two grown daughters.

About the Cartoonist

Barry Hunau is an editorial cartoonist in the San Francisco Bay Area. His cartoons appear in newspapers and on the editorial page of "The Jerusalem Post." Barry's cartoons have been included in several editions of "Best Editorial Cartoons of The Year." He is a member of The Association of American Editorial Cartoonists.